Contents

KV-646-783

Introduction

If you have chosen to work with 8–10s in your church, you don't need us to tell you that you have taken on a challenging task! Whilst you probably don't need to be convinced that children have a vital part to play in God's kingdom, you may have bought this book to be re-envisioned, encouraged and supported in the important work of discipleship and nurture you carry out faithfully, week after week. We all benefit from being trained, equipped and exposed to new ideas and we trust that you will find this book both practical and inspirational.

About the authors

You have come to this book with the expectation that it will help you in your ministry – so you will want to know that we, the authors, are qualified to offer you that help.

Firstly, we are parents, loving our children and taking our responsibility for them seriously. As Christian parents, we are given the responsibility of bringing up our children as members of the body of Christ. Increasingly, as they grow up, we need to trust other members of that body to share God's truth with them. As we have seen our own children grow, we have begun to recognise that children gradually move beyond the influence of simply their closest family. This is particularly true of the age group we are concerned with in this book. As parents, our desire is to see work with 8–10s in our churches that offers our children the kinds of learning and role models that will help them take the Christian faith seriously for themselves.

Secondly, we are teachers who have had many years of experience working in school with children in the 8–10 age group. We see them struggle to learn and make sense of the world they live in. We celebrate their successes with them, and seek to support them as they learn. Underpinning all that we do with them is our understanding of how they learn best. It is our desire to see how this understanding can support us, as we try to reach children in our churches.

Thirdly, we have worked with 8–10s and are in positions of leadership in our own church. This means we are challenged constantly about the crucial issues facing the church today. What will church be like in the 21st century? How can we work with people of all ages as we seek to share the gospel with our communities? While this book focuses specifically on the 8–10 age group, it is borne out of a desire to see the place of these children in the context of the whole kingdom of God. We hope that we will have helped you to keep this bigger perspective at the centre of your thinking too.

How to use this book

As we'll see in Chapter Three, we all learn differently: feel free to use this book in a number of ways. You can read it straight through from beginning to end, or dip in and out, referring to the chapters that meet your immediate need (although we hope you'll go back and read the others too!). You'll notice that the left-hand pages contain slightly more in-depth text, while the right-hand pages concentrate more on practical information and activities. These are designed to help you work through some of the issues raised on the left-hand page. Right-hand pages contain:

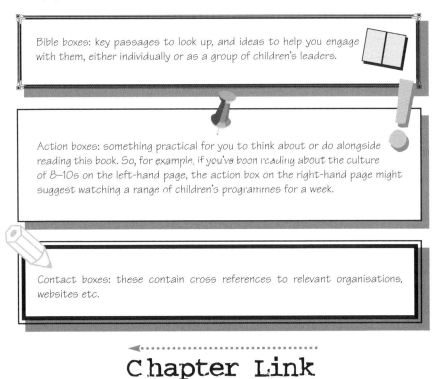

Bible boxes: key passages to look up, and ideas to help you engage with them, either individually or as a group of children's leaders.

Action boxes: something practical for you to think about or do alongside reading this book. So, for example, if you've been reading about the culture of 8–10s on the left-hand page, the action box on the right-hand page might suggest watching a range of children's programmes for a week.

Contact boxes: these contain cross references to relevant organisations, websites etc.

Chapter Link

Chapter links: to point you to other places in the book that deal with related issues.

These practical ideas can be used individually or as a group, so you can also use these right-hand pages as training resources for a number of children's leaders together.

CHILDREN AND THE WORLD

Chapter One – The Basis for our Work with Children

- So what do you need to know about working with 8–10s?
- What music do they like?
- Do they watch too much TV?
- How can you help them engage with the Bible?

These are the sort of questions we'll look at in later chapters, but this first chapter covers The Most Important Things to know about working with children of this age group – that God loves them, that they are created in his image, and that he has a plan for them.

When we read the Bible, it becomes clear that God has had a plan and purpose throughout history: to restore the people he created, so that they might have a right relationship with him. One of the most graphic illustrations of this rescue plan is in Exodus, where Moses led the nation of Israel out of slavery in Egypt. Did he lead only the adults? Of course not! The whole tribe of Israelites would have crossed the Red Sea, carrying their babies and holding the hands of their children. It was important to ensure that those children understood what had been done for them, so Moses gave specific instructions about celebrating Passover, in what is perhaps the first recorded syllabus for teaching children about God:

> After you have entered the country promised to you by the LORD, you and your children must continue to celebrate Passover each year. Your children will ask you 'What are we celebrating?' And you will answer, 'The Passover animal is killed to honour the LORD. We do these things because on that night long ago the LORD passed over the homes of our people in Egypt … [and] … saved our children from death' (Exodus 12:24–26).

The Bible makes it clear that God considers it vital that we provide for children in terms of letting them know the stories of God, and helping them to join in with the life of faith. Then, just as now, children were part of the community and therefore present at many of the key occasions of worship, and adults had a clear responsibility to answer their questions and teach them about God and all that he had done for them. The theme of believing adults having responsibility for the spiritual growth of their children occurs many times in the Old Testament – check out some of the Bible references opposite.

The story of the life of Samuel shows us that God can begin to work in a person's life before they are born, and in 1 Samuel 3 we see God choosing to speak to the child Samuel rather than Eli the priest. Look at the story of Naaman, in 2 Kings 5 to see how important the witness of a young girl could be. Children are able to relate to God and be used by him in working out his purposes.

For a really comprehensive look at the position of children in New Testament times and an examination of key related Bible passages and their cultural context, check out W A Strange, *Children in the Early Church*, Paternoster Press.

Children were important in the Old Testament, both because they continued a family line by inheriting land and property, and because they continued the faith of the nation.

> *You must be very careful not to forget the things you have seen God do for you. Keep reminding yourselves, and tell your children and grandchildren as well (Deuteronomy 4:9,10).*

> *Listen Israel! The LORD our God is the only true God! So love the LORD your God with all your heart, soul, and strength. Memorise his laws and tell them to your children over and over again. Talk about them all the time, whether you're at home or walking along the road or going to bed at night, or getting up in the morning … (Deuteronomy 6:4–7).*

> *…Each year the Israelites must come together to celebrate the Festival of Shelters at the place where the LORD chooses to be worshipped … Everyone must come – men, women, children, and even the foreigners who live in your towns. And each new generation will listen and learn to worship the LORD their God with fear and trembling and to do exactly what is said in God's Law (Deuteronomy 31:10–13).*

In the New Testament, the Word becomes flesh – Jesus is God with us. We see more clearly than ever before what God is like, and how he wants us to live. Many of the things Jesus said or did shocked those who considered themselves to be religious, and challenged them to think again. John reminds us at the end of his Gospel that there are many things Jesus did which are not recorded for us. Therefore those events and sayings which are recorded have particular significance, and it is surely even more significant that an encounter Jesus had with children occurs in three of the Gospels.

> *Some people brought their children to Jesus so that he could bless them by placing his hands on them. But his disciples told the people to stop bothering him.*
> *When Jesus saw this, he became angry and said, 'Let the children come to me! Don't try to stop them. People who are like these little children belong to the kingdom of God. I promise you that you cannot get into God's kingdom, unless you accept it the way a child does.' Then Jesus took the children in his arms and blessed them by placing his hands on them (Mark 10:13–16).*

Many thousands of words have been written about this passage and the corresponding ones in Luke 18 and Matthew 19. But there seem to be a few very obvious lessons we can learn:

- *Let the children come to me*
  Jesus wants children to come to him just as much as adults. This surprised those around him. Clearly, the culture of the time – as demonstrated by the disciples' actions – was to keep children separate. Jesus shows that God sent his Son to be the Saviour of the world – including the world's children – and his disciples are to do all they can to help those children approach him.
- *Don't try to stop them*
  As we've seen in the Old Testament, adults have a clear responsibility towards helping children grow in the life of faith. Here, we are exhorted to ensure that we do not let anything get in the way of children meeting Jesus. Compare the behaviour of the disciples, which angered Jesus, with his own words and actions. Jesus has already spoken clearly to his disciples about their attitude towards children: 'When you welcome even a child because of me, you welcome me. And when you welcome me, you welcome the one who sent me' (Mark 9:37). He makes it quite clear that God does not look favourably on those who obstruct or hinder a child's relationship with him (Mark 9:42).
- *We can learn truth from children*
  In fact, there may be truths that we can only learn from children: '...you cannot get into God's kingdom, unless you accept it the way a child does' (verse 15).

At your next leaders' meeting, start with a time of imaginative prayer. Read the passage from Mark 10, and ask people to use their imaginations to become part of the scene. Perhaps they can see themselves as a parent who brings their child to Jesus, or as one of the disciples trying to keep control and order. Encourage them to imagine the feel of the grass beneath their feet, the weather on that day and in particular how they feel about the things that happen. Afterwards, invite people to share what new insights the exercise gave them into Jesus' words, the children or themselves.

Ron Buckland in *Children and the Gospel* (SU, 2001) has a chapter entitled 'Jesus about children' where he looks in more detail at the Mark 10 passage and its parallels in Matthew's and Luke's Gospels. Buckland points out that this passage is about adults as well as children. Jesus says that children already belong to the kingdom of God, and challenges adults to discover a childlike faith.

Francis Bridger in *Children Finding Faith* (SU, 2000) gives a very helpful study of another passage in Mark's Gospel where Jesus meets children – Mark 9:36,37 – see the section 'Jesus and Children' (p130). Francis Bridger warns that the Bible passages where Jesus met children are not always straightforward, and we should be careful not to read into them our own meanings. He concludes from this passage in Mark, as we have seen reinforced in the verses from Mark 10, that Jesus commends children to our loving care, and teaches that children can be representatives of God, teaching us all about God's kingdom.

Some of the other occasions when Jesus met or talked about children are listed below. In each case, consider:
- What was Jesus' attitude to children?
- What was the attitude of those he was talking to?
- How does the passage suggest we should treat children?

a Matthew 18:1–7
b Matthew 18:10,11
c Matthew 21:15,16

It is worth spending time with this passage, and this picture of Jesus. Before we rush off to plan next week's programme, worry about the content of the First Aid box or panic about how to discipline effectively, we need to sit at the feet of the one in whose name we work, and ask for his Spirit to fill us again with his love for these children.

Alongside the God-given responsibility of teaching children about him – both what he has done and how we should respond – comes the joy of worshipping God together. Having children and adults worshipping together is not just a good idea for children, as they learn from the words and actions of those around them, but also for the adults too. The old adage that 'children should be seen and not heard' is not how things should be in God's family.

When asked to describe the ideal conditions for worship, one person replied, 'First, I would sedate all the children!' Whilst this remark raises an understanding smile from some, it isn't a positive picture of how we can worship together as a church family. Actually, although there aren't many examples, there are a few passages in the Bible that specifically show us God's people – young and old – gathering as a family and actively participating in worship together. Nehemiah 8:1–6 tells us that:

> '…Ezra the priest came with the Law and stood before the crowd of men, women, and the children who were old enough to understand. From early morning until midday, he read the Law of Moses to them, and they listened carefully … the people shouted 'Amen! Amen!' Then they bowed down with their faces to the ground and worshipped the Lord.'

In biblical times, it's very likely that children were present on many occasions of worship – they were just part of the family, and where their parents went, they would have followed.

Similarly, in the New Testament, we can surmise that – with the family unit still foundational – children would have been part of the life of the Christian community. Paul's challenge to the New Testament Christians in Galatians 3:28 – to live and work out church as an inclusive body that values all its members equally, 'whether you are a Jew or a Greek, a slave or a free person, a man or a woman' also challenges us about how we value everyone in our Christian family, whatever their age.

It's worth noting briefly here that there are questions about the level of responsibility that children's workers can or should take, as non-parents, for a child's spiritual growth. For example, what is a parent's responsibility in a child's life, as contrasted with that of other adults? For the nation of Israel, there would probably have been a different understanding of corporate responsibility, arising from a sense of community that's unfamiliar to us today. Today we no longer input into the lives of other people's children in quite the same way, and the values of community in our society have dwindled. We need to work through the implications of this for our work with children – especially those coming from unbelieving homes. We know that whilst in biblical times, children were predominantly brought up and instructed in faith in the context of the family, this is not the norm today. Many of the children we encounter in our groups today come from a variety of home situations, where faith may or may not be seen as important.

What do you think about this? Talk about this with your leadership team. How, as a church, can we recapture that sense of biblical community and model it to others?

Chapter Link

Many churches wrestle with the issue of how to include children in worship, and while we can begin to learn principles from studying the Bible, it is up to us to work out how to apply those principles to our situation today. In Chapter Five we look at how to pray, read the Bible and worship with the 8–10 age group, and how this could be part of what is going on in the whole church.

So, how does all this inform our work with 8–10s today? It means that in obedience to God we will seek to grow children's awareness – in ways that are appropriate to their age and development – that God is real and that he cares very deeply for them. We will want to teach them about him, about the history of his relationship with his people, about his character and priorities and about Jesus. We will be prepared to be creative about how we do this – look at the varied ways the Israelites passed on teaching about God (see the passages on page 7 from Deuteronomy). Interestingly, they used ritual, drama, role-play, songs, celebration etc – all things that are highly enjoyable for 8–10s!

It is not our responsibility to get children into heaven – that is the work of the Holy Spirit, made possible by the death of Jesus. But if we are working with 8–10s, it is our responsibility to make sure that they have heard the good news which God offers them in Jesus, and to assist them in growing an ongoing relationship with him, as they truly learn what it is to be a disciple of Christ today.

Some children will come to us already sure of God's love for them and their place in his plan; some will come knowing stories about Noah, Jonah and Jesus, but unsure what it means to them; some will come with little more than a vague realisation that God is out there somewhere; and some will not even have that. Our responsibility is clearly to teach them, for how can they respond to a God they do not know? And it is also to encourage them to make responses to God as they get to know him. As well as offering them the opportunity to make specific responses to Christ, we should be helping them to work that out in individual decisions on a regular basis. Our children will be making choices every day – small choices about friends, homework and hobbies which, put together, shape them into the people they are. So it is also the small choices they make as they encounter Jesus which build into a life lived for him, or a life which rejects him. Every time we speak or act in Jesus' name, the children around us will be making their response. We need to understand how faith develops in children of this age, so that we avoid pressurising them into making a response which they are not ready for, but also avoid missing encouraging signs of growth, or becoming discouraged because the children don't seem 'spiritual' enough.

Two people who have done significant work on faith development are James Fowler and John Westerhoff, and their ideas are summarised over the next few pages.

John Westerhoff (*Will Our Children Have Faith?*, Moorhouse Publishing, 2000) has written about his developmental view of faith and conversion. He identifies four stages, which are achieved and passed through as someone grows up in the Christian faith:

1 Experienced faith
For a young child in a Christian family, their understanding of faith will be what they experience. They are learning about love and trust. Believing in God will be just what everyone around them does.

2 Affiliative faith
As children grow older, start school and become more aware of the community outside their own family, they have a strong sense of wanting to belong. They need to be part of a community or group, valued and accepted. They may accept Jesus because of what he represents to them – becoming part of a group, with clear guidelines about what behaviour is acceptable, and often a group ethos expressed through uniform, songs or games.

3 Searching faith
The child is becoming more independent, and asking questions. Rather than accepting the norms of family, community or church, children think about things for themselves, sometimes experimenting with alternative answers. This stage is often associated with adolescence, and Westerhoff argues that only now does the child begin to have a commitment to personal faith.

4 Owned faith
This is the end of the conversion process, which may have taken many years or may occur quite quickly. The child is now an older teenager or adult, who knows they have a personal relationship with Jesus.

As you read these definitions, do you find them helpful? Do they fit with your experiences? What limitations do you think they have?

On a large piece of paper, draw a road stretching from one side to the other. One end represents being far from God, knowing nothing about him and living a life which disobeys him. The other end represents living a perfect life, loving God absolutely and doing everything he asks. (Only Jesus made it here on earth – but we'll all get there in heaven!) Where would you put yourself? Can you identify times in your life when you have been travelling in the wrong direction, stopped and sat down or run ahead, making great progress? Where would you put the members of your group on the road? Ask God to help you encourage each one to keep travelling in the right direction.

Fowler, Nipkow, Schweitzer (editors), *Stages of Faith and Religious Development*, SCM, 1992; Francis Bridger, *Children Finding Faith*, SU, 2000

According to Westerhoff's stages, most of our 8 to 10-year-olds will belong to the 'affiliative' faith stage. We should be aware that the norms of the group will have a great influence on them, and be careful not to abuse this. For example, if we have a time of prayer, make sure that everyone has the option of not joining in. We can use the love this age group has for stories to share with them the great narrative passages of the Bible, and begin to help them see how their own life story fits into God's plan. But we should not be surprised if they are not very reflective – if we impose times of meditation on them, we may find that they are just saying what they think we want to hear. Some people argue that these limitations in children's faith development mean they should not be expected to use the gifts of the Holy Spirit, such as tongues and healing, and you should talk this through with the leadership of your church to find out their position.

We should also be aware that there will be some in our groups who still have only a primitive faith, whatever their age. We need to nurture carefully those who have what seems a simple, intuitive or emotional response to stories etc. Rather than dismissing such children as having no faith, we need to recognise that they are on a faith journey too. Jesus commends a child-like faith to his disciples, and often did great things for those with only the most basic faith.

In our desire to work with children aged from 8 to 10, we have a clear biblical mandate. Throughout the Bible we have seen an unequivocal message:

- God loves children.
- His plan for salvation includes them.
- They are part of the church, worshipping, growing and learning.
- Adults, in particular their parents, have a God-given responsibility to teach them about the life of faith.
- As they grow up, children need to decide for themselves about believing in God.

As children's leaders, we have a responsibility to God, and towards the children with whom we work. Our responsibility to God starts with listening to him - to his love for all those he created, and his longing that we should all know him. Let's be clear about the place of children in God's heart, so that he can trust us with the precious task of caring for them.

Our responsibility to the children perhaps also ought to start with listening – listening to their experience of the world, and to their longings and fears. As adults, so often we rush to tell them things. Maybe it's time to let them tell us a few things first! So before we look at how we might teach them, we spend some time in the next few chapters examining the world of the 8 to 10-year-old.

James Fowler has written about seven stages of faith. He is concerned with faith in an abstract way, regardless of what the focus of that faith is, so his definitions are harder to apply directly than Westerhoff's! To make them more concrete, let's imagine how they might apply to a child who was exploring faith in God.

1 Primal faith

A basic experience of trust, based on the infant's experience of trusting their parents. A baby knows that being left in the crèche is OK, because someone will look after them, and that Mum or Dad will be back to collect them.

2 Intuitive-projective faith

A growing awareness of the protective and threatening powers surrounding them. The young child is stimulated by stories, gestures and symbols. Young children love singing songs they know, and hearing stories about Jesus.

3 Mythic-literal faith

Here's where our 8–10s might fit. The child is beginning to think logically, and beginning to order the world. The immediate community is important, and the child learns more about stories, symbols and attitudes. They understand that goodness is rewarded and badness punished. The child likes to belong to a group, and if the group pray easily or sings worship songs enthusiastically, they are happy to join in. They pick up values from their family, so if the family is Christian they may have a good understanding of the Christian faith.

4 Synthetic-conventional faith

Typically reached in adolescence, where personal experience reaches beyond the family and becomes more reflective. The teenager becomes more critical of beliefs they have previously taken on-board. Sometimes this leads to rebellion, or to a personal reaffirmation of faith. Teenage Christians can be very dogmatic and intolerant of perceived weakness or hypocrisy, but also very excited about their faith and its possibilities.

5 Individuative-reflective faith

The young person assumes greater responsibility for their personal beliefs and attitudes. They can understand the perspective of others, and begin to make commitments in relationships and vocation. The young adult is secure in their Christian faith, and makes decisions about work, sexuality and serving God, on the basis of the Bible and prayer.

6 Conjunctive faith

By mid-life, a person recognises that life cannot be fitted into a tidy conceptual scheme, and accepts tension and paradox. A Christian grows in wisdom, love, self-control and all the fruit of the Spirit. They often take on some responsibility in the church, whether in small groups, prayer partnerships or leadership.

7 Universalising faith

Only attained by a few in their maturity. Persons are grounded and secure, working selflessly for the values of love and justice. These are the saints in the church, who we look to for their wisdom, humility and service to God.

Chapter Two – Growing Pains

What's a tweenager?

The word 'tweenager' seems to be used by the media and marketing organisations to describe a child who is not yet a teenager, ie 13 or older, but who behaves like one! So according to these sources, our 8, 9 and 10-year-olds are typical 'tweenagers'. To the manufacturers' delight, they now have some money of their own and certainly a big influence over how their parents or carers spend their money. Many pop bands, TV shows or fashion styles will be aimed at this age group, who are the 21st century's newest consumers. The rest of us look on and shudder, muttering about the loss of childhood, the end of innocence and the exploitation of our children. Even in churches, many people are put off working with this age group because they appear to be becoming increasingly sophisticated, discerning and demanding. We worry that if we are not cool enough, they will not want to know.

We will look at the pressures that surround children of this age later on: at their response to these pressures and at how real this media picture of them is. But let's focus on some of the children themselves.

What are today's children like?

Let's peep through the kitchen windows of some imaginary houses in Britain in the 21st century. They are interesting houses for us, because each one includes a child between the ages of 8 and 10. These are not real children, but they could be. Their family backgrounds, their favourite bands and their taste in clothes are shared by many very real children, but in some cases they are stereotypes, imagined as a way into the world of today's children.

Home background

The first house is a large four-bedroomed detached house, in a quiet cul-de-sac. Alix bursts into the kitchen, and throws her bookbag on the table – a letter from the rural Church of England primary school she attends hangs out of it. Alix is 8, and has a younger sister. She is white, and lives with her mother. Her mother has driven her and her sister home from school, and spends much of the week driving them to swimming lessons, piano lessons, French club and out to friends for tea. She works part time at the local college of further education. Every other Friday, Alix's dad's partner picks her up from school, and she spends the weekend with her dad and his family. She has two older stepbrothers, who are the sons of her dad's partner. Alix would like to be a bridesmaid, and hopes that her dad will get married soon. Her dad's house is surrounded by countryside, and at the weekends she can go horse riding. She loves animals, and would like a rabbit as a pet. Her favourite books are Lucy Dale's 'Animal Ark' series.

We used this personal profile to find about some of the 8–10s we've worked with during the writing of this book. Use it with one or more of the children you work with to find out what matters to them.

My personal profile

My name is:

I am ___ years old

The most important thing you need to know about me is:

If I could choose what to do on Saturday I would:

If I had a hundred pounds I would:

The person I would most like to meet is:

Because:

The things I like doing least are:

Some things that worry me are:

Author Nick Harding surveyed nearly 1,000 9 to 11-year-olds about their schools, homes and relationships and about what they see and hear through TV, music and books. Check out his conclusions in *Kids' Culture* (SU, 2003).

The second house is a suburban semi. Round the back is a well-worn stretch of grass, where Ben and his friends are playing football. Ben is 9, the middle boy of a family of three. He is black, his grandparents being of Afro-Caribbean origin. Both his mum and dad were born and brought up in Britain, and have been married for 15 years. They are committed members of the local church, and Ben will be going to the youth club at church later. He has walked home from his large junior school with his friend, after a school football match. His mum is at home, but she doesn't have the car during the week because his dad needs it for work. He often uses his skateboard to get around, and wishes his mum would let him go out on his own more.

It starts to rain, so Ben and his friend rush indoors to get on the PlayStation before his brother gets in from secondary school. Ben's mum will make them some tea, before they take his friend home. Then she will probably make him read to her, although he would rather watch TV. He likes the Cartoon Network and *The Simpsons*.

The third window belongs to a flat, and there is nobody at home. Cherise, who is 10, is out with her gran, doing the shopping. Her gran has swollen ankles and needs Cherise to help push the trolley round. Cherise is in Year Six at school, and tonight her gran should be at an open evening about choosing secondary schools, but Cherise has forgotten to remind her and there is no-one who could look after Cherise anyway. Cherise dawdles past the display of hair accessories and nail varnish, wondering when her gran will give her some pocket money. When she sees her dad, he gives her a lot of money, but it's only once every few months. Her mum is very young, and sometimes comes round to help Cherise paint her nails, but she's getting married soon, so is too busy at the moment. Cherise hopes her gran might buy her a magazine – she can't read very well, but likes the pictures of Atomic Kitten and S Club 8.

When or where might Alix, Ben and Cherise hear about Jesus?

If they came to a holiday club you were running, where would you start?

How much do you think they would know about the Bible or about Jesus?

Look at the material you use with young people (for example, think about language, illustrations, examples and stories you use).

Are there assumptions made in the material which would feel hurtful or exclusive to any of these children? Are there concepts or ideas they would not understand?

Characteristics of 8 to 10-year-olds

Spiritually

8 to 10-year-olds have a clear sense of right and wrong. Their ideas are still quite black and white, and they have a keen sense of justice. They are able to make decisions about their own actions, and understand the consequences of those decisions. They can begin to understand the idea of God being Trinity, and relate well to Jesus, as God made flesh. They are beginning to understand and make sense of things such as Jesus' death and resurrection, and in some church traditions can start to receive Communion. However, they may not be able to completely order these things in their minds, or give a concrete reason for their faith if asked. They can decide to follow Jesus, but further steps of commitment may also be taken as they progress through childhood. They still have a great capacity for imagination, awe and wonder and a lively spiritual curiosity. Family faith and values are still very important in influencing children of this age.

How are they growing? – physical development

Cherise is fast approaching puberty. Her gran is unaware of this, because for her generation it wasn't until they were teenagers that their periods started, and 'puberty' wasn't much talked about anyway – but Cherise's body is changing, her moods are swinging, she is thinking about boys and feels quite confused about her emotions. The boys in her class at school are mostly smaller than the girls and are not as developed physically, but one of the girls has already started her periods and many of them now wear a bra. The magazines they read give explicit advice about sex, and they watch soap operas on TV where the characters all have physical relationships. They talk confidently about how far they have gone with their boyfriends, and Cherise is not astute enough to see how much of this is boasting. She worries about how much she eats, because she knows that it's only thin girls who get a boyfriend, and sometimes if her gran has given her a big tea she will go and be sick in the toilet. She envies her Mum's skill with make-up and trendy clothes, and wants to be like her.

Ben spends a lot of time playing sport – particularly football – so that he is fit and strong. He will eat loads of crisps and sweets if he can get away with it. He already has two fillings, before he has even lost all of his milk teeth. He goes out on his bike at weekends with his dad and elder brother, and desperately wants to keep up, so is always pushing himself to do better. Sometimes he gets up early and does press-ups in his bedroom. He doesn't spend too much time worrying about what he looks like, although he does like to gel his hair before school. One of his gang of friends is a girl who likes playing football, but he has no time for the girls who sit around in groups giggling and talking about 'girls' stuff'.

Alix is losing her puppy fat, and beginning to grow taller and slimmer. She has long legs and long glossy hair. She has recently mastered riding a bike, although she doesn't have much time to ride it. She used to go to ballet, which has given her good posture and graceful movement. She enjoys dancing, and will often involuntarily skip along or make up a little dance. She spends a lot of time out of doors at the weekend with her dad, and goes horse riding there. Her mother is quite strict about her diet, making sure she gets plenty of fresh fruit and vegetables and not letting her eat sweets, so she has clear skin and healthy teeth and hair.

She enjoys swimming, and has just started to be self-conscious about getting changed, preferring to be in a cubicle. Her school encourages boys and girls to mix and work together, and Alix has no problem with boys. She has few friends who are boys, because they are not interested in the same things. She has done a project at school about healthy lifestyles, and is currently fired-up with enthusiasm for plenty of exercise and a healthy diet, but her interest will soon wane.

Characteristics of 8 to 10-year-olds

Physically

They have mastered many basic skills and are now starting to develop advanced, sometimes specialised skills. They may show an interest and aptitude for a particular sport, developing speed, stamina, fitness and agility, or they may begin to play a musical instrument, developing creativity, musical expression and technical ability. They can build, paint, manipulate and enjoy constructing intricate pictures and models, sometimes using Lego, Airfix or commercial figures, but often using household objects and craft materials too. (Many children of this age have particularly skilful thumbs and quick reaction times, due no doubt to the hours they spend on their Gameboys and PlayStations!) In terms of physical and emotional changes as they approach puberty, it will be noticeable that girls are developing more quickly than boys.

There are lots of good websites designed for children to use, full of information about health. Some useful addresses:

www.bbc.co.uk/health/kids

www.healthykids.org.uk

www.kidshealth.org

'Periods are hard to get used to. When you start you could be mad, sad, cranky – different people have different ways of adjusting to it. In the end, you will get used to it.'

Eliza, aged 11

What do they feel? – emotional development

Ben has a good relationship with his parents, and this helps him feel good about himself. They have been there for him consistently, and as he gets older he finds himself being good friends with his parents, especially with his dad. They enjoy kicking a football around in the garden, and his dad knows not to go on at him too much. Sometimes his mum wants to talk to him about his day at school or his friends, which makes Ben impatient. He doesn't spend much time thinking about himself, he prefers doing things. He thinks he might soon be too old for his mum to kiss him goodbye at school, although he's not sure how to tell her. But he doesn't want his friends to think he's a bit soft, and their opinion is becoming increasingly important to him.

He is aware that the colour of his skin makes him different, and some of the boys who are jealous of his place in the football team will call him names. But he doesn't take it too seriously, and has lots of posters of black footballers on his walls at home. His older brother has had real problems at secondary school, and his mum and dad have had to go in to see the staff. There's no way Ben wants all that fuss about him, so even if someone does call him a name he doesn't tell his parents about it. He will stick up for others though, and once got into a fight when someone called one of his friends a 'Paki'.

Alix knows that she is loved by both her mum and her dad, but does wonder why they don't love each other any more. Her dad seems very happy with his new life, and Alix loves going to visit him at weekends. The atmosphere at his house is very relaxed, and her older stepbrothers tease her or spoil her in turn. She doesn't have to worry about how anyone else is feeling. But at home, her mum is sometimes upset. Alix knows when she has been crying, even though her mum never talks about it and will pretend to be cheerful.

Alix finds that hard, and tiptoes around, not sure how she is supposed to behave. Sometimes she wishes she could live at her dad's all the time, and then she feels awful because she loves her mum and feels responsible for her in some way. Her younger sister is naughty and often has tantrums, which give Alix's mum a headache. Then Alix feels as though it is her fault for not looking after her sister. Alix seems to have everything materially, but is often a confused and worried little girl.

Characteristics of 8 to 10-year-olds

Emotionally

They increasingly need to be accepted by their peer group, and if this doesn't happen they can be bullied and experience isolation and loneliness. Popular children can be powerful figures, attracting a loyal following of others keen to be in the right crowd. They are beginning to find their own identity, and they can be moody or defy authority. They can also be energetic, creative, sensitive and thoughtful. They clearly distinguish fantasy from reality, no longer believing in Father Christmas, for example, and also seeing through platitudes or inadequate explanations. They are aware of the emotions of others, and can feel responsible for them, for example in the case of a parent who is upset. They are often given extra responsibilities, from organising their school bag and homework to looking after a pet or a younger sibling. They take pride in something done well, and respond well to praise.

'They are still quite naïve and forming their own thoughts and opinions about life and their world. They are still quite immature and lacking in self-confidence – this can be a good and bad thing; it means they are sometimes quite clingy!'

Parent of 8-year-old girl

'My child fluctuates in his feelings about himself and life in general. I worry about his own self-concept at times, and sometimes the evidence of low self-esteem.'

Parent of 8-year-old boy

Cherise is becoming increasingly aware that it's a bit odd to live with your gran, and her reaction to this is to become cheeky and sometimes defiant towards her. She finds her gran is unable to discipline her, so she often gets her own way. She has always found school work difficult, and tends to switch off during lessons. She built up a good relationship with one of the teaching assistants, who she would see regularly for special needs support, but she doesn't think her teacher likes her. She often feels invisible at school, ignored by her classmates and overlooked by the teacher. She dreams of being whisked away one day in a stretch limo by someone famous, making everyone wish they had made more time for her.

What do they like to do?

Alix loves music and dancing. She is not very sophisticated in her tastes, and is just as likely to sing playground rhymes or do the actions to the 'Hokey-Cokey' as know the words to the current Number One. She and her friends learn clapping rhymes in the playground, and sing while they skip. She likes watching children's programmes on TV with her younger sister, and still plays with Barbie. If she buys a comic, she likes the 'pets page' and the stories about Cinderella or Sleeping Beauty. Her mum took Alix and her sister to a ballet at Christmas, and she was enchanted by the costumes, the scenery and the dancing. She has lots of Disney videos, retelling famous fairy stories, and dreams of being a princess when she grows up.

Her mum finds the idea of her growing up difficult, and recently visited the school to complain about the content of their Sex Education Programme. She doesn't like Alix to play with make-up, and thinks many of the clothes available for girls of her age are 'tarty'. Alix loves her mum and wants to please her, but sometimes wishes she could do the things her friends do. She is trying to persuade her mum to let her have a sleepover at her house.

Characteristics of 8–10 year-olds

Mentally

They are able to think about people, places and times beyond their own immediate experience. They can see other points of view, and empathise with others. They respect expertise, and are eager to learn, both in school and out. There is beginning to be a difference in attitude and achievement between boys and girls in school, particularly in reading and writing. They can transfer skills to new situations, and think creatively to solve problems. They can exhibit a high level of knowledge and expertise in an area of particular interest (this age group is a key one for crazes!), and may join a club, subscribe to a magazine or use the Internet to further personal interests.

'They are so interesting and fun to be with. They respond well to praise and encouragement.'
Parent of 10-year-old boy

'Great thinking age, new ideas, idealism, enthusiasm, not yet spoiled by cynicism!'
Junior school teacher

Ben loves football: when he's not playing it, he watches it on TV or plays football games on the PlayStation. He is fortunate to be good at football, which gives him a lot of prestige among his friends. They have nothing to do with boys who don't play football, and can sometimes be cruel to boys who want to play but are not very skilful. Ben hasn't got much time for reading, but knows vast amounts of information about the team he supports, and will look at the sports pages of his dad's newspaper to read the match reports. He doesn't like singing, and mumbles his way through assembly at school. It's not cool to sing – unless you are at a match, of course.

It's becoming important to Ben to work out what is acceptable behaviour among his friends and how to fit in – he is popular at the moment, but is aware of how allegiances can change. He wants to wear trainers to school, and can't see why his mum won't let him. It becomes so important to him that he takes his trainers in a bag and changes as soon as his mum is out of sight. Ben loves the *Star Wars* films, and will often watch bits of them on video with his dad, who's also a fan. He has some *Star Wars* Lego, and on wet days will build complex models. Some of his friends have got kits that include motors and lights as well, but Ben hasn't got the patience to sit for hours connecting wires up. He likes to have a huge battle with his spaceships and smash them all up!

Cherise spends hours daydreaming, which often gets her into trouble at school. In her dreams she is slim, beautiful and popular, and going out with Gareth Gates. In real life she can never think of something to say, and is aware that she doesn't have many friends. She often spends lunchtime talking to the dinner ladies, rather than be faced with her loneliness. She knows her gran doesn't have much money, but she wishes she could buy her some more up-to-date clothes. She loves the times when her mum comes round, because she'll often bring her some clothes she doesn't want any more. Cherise will spend hours in her room trying clothes, new hairstyles and make-up.

One of the girls at school seems to want to be friends with her, and has told her how easy it is to get what you want from shops without paying. Cherise is not sure about this, but she is desperate to get 'in with the crowd'. She watches lots of the soaps on TV, so she can talk about them the next day. Sometimes she dreams about living in one of them.

Characteristics of 8 to 10-year-olds

Socially

They are beginning to branch out from their immediate family, and other relationships are becoming increasingly important. Friendships are developing, usually single-sex at this age. They often form gangs, clubs or teams, based on shared interests such as pop music or football. They may invent passwords, rituals and in-jokes that strengthen the identity of the group. They increasingly control their own social life, rather than relying on parents to make friends for them. They use the telephone, mobile phone and e-mail to keep in touch, arranging their own visits, parties and sleepovers.

'They are beginning to form personalities of their own. They are becoming individual and changing all the time. They are inquisitive about every aspect of life. They are very aware of right and wrong, and fairness.'

Parent of 8 and 10-year-old boys

'From 8 years old onwards, children continually develop individuality, their own opinions, and can work in an increasingly independent manner. They seem less dependent emotionally.'

Junior school teacher

Our response

Of course, Ben, Cherise and Alix are stereotypes, but we will all recognise some things from the descriptions about them. They have a lot to teach us about the world of 8–10s today. And whilst there are some great things about being a child of this age, perhaps more than ever before, these children have to deal with a complex world and its associated pressures. These are the kinds of children we will meet in our work with this age group and we need to know what goes on in their world.

As we shall see in a moment, it is perfectly possible to present a depressing picture of the world our 8–10s inhabit. We shall necessarily look at issues such as divorce, abuse, bullying and poverty, and see that these things are the very real issues that many children face daily. But the picture is not all gloomy. The good news is that children are amazingly resilient. We have worked with children such as the 9-year-old boy who came to school each day having prepared clothes and lunchboxes for a younger sibling, leaving at home a mother too drunk to do these things for them; and a 10-year-old girl who acts as carer to two disabled parents on top of her daily schooling. Yet these children, given the stable environment of a school that cares about them, could still be children, messing about with their friends, playing hide-and-seek or having a good kick-around in the playground. However hard society tries to rob them of it, deep down children still seem to want their childhood, and there is hope.

We have seen the concerns and pleasures adults have in their relationships with children, but what about the children themselves? Their comments opposite show clearly what an 'in-between' stage in their lives our 8–10s are at. They still have simple childlike fears, alongside the 'big issues' that society throws at them. The most important things they want us to know about them are straightforward and honest, but the people they would most like to meet are almost exclusively the sports and pop stars who inhabit the world of the magazines and television programmes they encounter. Suddenly the label 'tweenagers' makes perfect sense. Children of this age group are not entirely sure whether it's still okay to be children or not!

When we asked the children these questions, the war in Afghanistan was making headlines on the television news and in the papers. Perhaps if we had done the interview during the subsequent summer holiday, the abduction and murder of two 10-year old girls in Cambridgeshire may well have influenced the response to the question, 'What worries you?' Children of this age read the papers and watch the news, and what they read and hear undoubtedly affects them.

We asked some children to fill in a personal profile. These are some of the things they said:

'Some things that worry me are…'
    '…when I die.'
    '…the dark.'
    '…wetting the bed.'
    '…Mum and Dad having arguments, in case they divorce.'
    '…that my work isn't good enough.
    '…the war between America and Afghanistan.'
    '…SATS [the Statutory Assessment Tests taken at the end of primary school] and tests.'

'The most important thing you need to know about me is…'
    '…that I'm a Christian.'
    '…that I love my mum and dad.'
    '…that I'm sometimes silly.'

'The person I would most like to meet is…'
    '…God, to know if he's real or not.'
    '…Michael Jackson. I want to question him on why he wanted plastic surgery on his face and why he didn't like what he looked like.'

Other people they wanted to meet included:
    JK Rowling (author of the Harry Potter books)
    David Beckham (football star)
    S-Club (pop band)
    …and many other sports and pop stars too!

The Media – fuelling fears?

Television

Ask your group of 8–10s how many of them watch *Eastenders* and the chances are a significant number of hands will go up. As a programme that is on before the watershed, and can be watched in omnibus on a Sunday afternoon, this is hardly surprising. So let's look at some facts about the programme, identified in a recent report from the National Family and Parenting Institute (NFPI). In one month's broadcasts children watching would have seen:

- episodes of domestic violence, including a husband throwing plates and a woman scratching her violent ex-husband
- death threats
- a woman punching a man
- a pub brawl
- three couples involved in extra-marital affairs
- the adoption of a teenage mother's child

From Getting into a Lather – Family Life in Britain's Soaps, NFPI, 2002

As Christians, we must believe that it matters if our children are watching programmes with this kind of content. They give the impression that family breakdown is inevitable and, as the report points out, portray characters whose social status is earned by anti-social behaviour.

'Parents do not bring up their children in isolation, and the media has a huge effect on what they feel, believe and fear.'
Mary MacLeod, Chief Executive of the NFPI, Press Release, 17 October, 2002

The problem is that such media portrayals give a wholly inaccurate picture to children who are at an age when they are not yet skilled at detecting such manipulation. Couples head around 75 per cent of families in Britain; the figure in Eastenders was just 40 per cent. Conflict between children and parents is universally badly handled in the soaps, and yet as another NFPI report highlights, most parents believe that the key to successful family life lies in time spent together and talking together (*The Millennial Family*, NFPI 1999). This is hardly the message children get from soap opera viewing!

Books

What about the books that Ben, Cherise, Alix and others like them enjoy reading? Jacqueline Wilson is one of the top children's authors of the moment, particularly amongst girls - and with good reason. Her books almost always centre on a child with a far from typical family background. One of her more famous heroines, Tracey Beaker, lives in a children's home. Many of her characters come from a single parent home, and many of the plots are all about how a child copes with a parent who also has a lot of growing up to do. Her witty, no-nonsense style gives humour to the sometimes desperate situations of her characters.

During the course of a week, watch a range of children's programmes aimed at 8–10s. What kinds of messages do they give about:

- the family?
- issues that matter to children?
- pressures they face?

Go into a bookshop or library, and ask the same questions of a selection of books on offer for 8–10s.

Few of us can be unaware of the Harry Potter phenomenon. The eponymous hero is an orphan, whose parents both died when he was a baby and who is forced to live a miserable life as an unwanted addition to the family of his aunt and uncle. The 'normal' family of Aunt Petunia and Uncle Vernon and their ghastly son Dudley is portrayed as quite undesirable, and Harry finds the support, friendship and acceptance he needs from his friends and the school community he joins. He still has deep longings for a family of his own, which become obvious when he sees his mother and father in a magical mirror, and he is delighted when a very unconventional godfather appears. The Harry Potter books have become a phenomenon for all sorts of reasons, but it is interesting to see the images they give of family, and to wonder whether part of their success is the fact that Harry's family or lack of it strikes chords with many of his readers. The author herself was a single parent when writing, who presumably saw no need to perpetuate the 'mum, dad and 2.4 kids' myth about family life.

As a literary device, of course the absence of responsible parents in fiction means that the children can be freed-up to go 'adventuring' (Blyton's Famous Five series is the perfect example). But for others, particularly more modern authors, a difficult family situation is not a device but the very issue the book confronts. And so, time after time in their reading, children are confronted with images of family life that make dysfunctional families the norm.

As we shall see in a moment, these are all realistic pressures that children might and do face in their lives. Authors like Jacqueline Wilson face up to the issues and portray the kinds of resilient children we talked about earlier dealing with these situations and coming out on top. Children need books like this, because exploring real issues through fiction is a powerful tool for helping children to deal with their emotions. But problem families make for better drama than happy ones, and we need to help children see that these kinds of situations aren't inevitable. To do this we need to know the facts. As we shall see, the truth is that the family unit is much harder to define than it once was, and that there are children in all our communities for whom family life is a struggle.

Consider how you teach young people about God.

Do you use words like 'God the Father'? Do you use images of fatherhood to help teach concepts of love and care? What problems might these cause for a child who has a less positive relationship with their father?

How do you feel about using language which describes God as a Mother?

Look carefully at the version of the Bible you use with your group, the words of songs you sing and the ideas in the teaching programme. Which use ideas about God that are timeless and true, and which use language or imagery that is culturally dependent and maybe not helpful to some in your group?

Read Matthew 12:46–50 and Matthew 10:35–37.

Jesus' words about earthly families seem harsh. How are we to understand them? (Look up John 19:26,27 to see Jesus' tenderness to his mother.)

Do they give any hope to someone who does not find the security and love they need from their earthly family?

Magazines

If television and fiction can be seen to give a somewhat distorted image of real life by focusing on the negatives, what about the magazines aimed at this age group? *Girl Talk* is aimed at a readership of girls who fall into the 8–10 age group. In one typical issue we found an animal page giving advice on pets and information on foxes, plus another page later on advertising membership of the RSPCA. Two other pages included puzzles and instructions for making a bead necklace. But by far the majority of the magazine's content and advertisements focused on the glamorous lifestyles of pop and television stars, giving advice on how to look and dress just like them.

Our response

In one sense there is nothing wrong with a bit of escapism, and we would be lying if we said that none of us had ever dreamed of a rich and famous lifestyle when we were younger. But the content of this magazine and others like it highlights the 'tweenager' dilemma. As society comes to terms with the fact that children reach puberty at an earlier age than they used to, so the marketing industry cashes in. These young consumers are confronted in magazines and on the television with images of clothes, make-up and teenage pop bands that seek to dress and treat children as mini-adults.

Suddenly we have moved away from harmless escapism, and into a world where we are in danger of robbing our 8–10s of their childhood. At the same time as both children and adults are seduced by such marketing ploys, we are increasingly denying them the kinds of activities that were once identified with childhood (see the Action box opposite).

Take, for example, a survey jointly undertaken by the Children's Society and the Children's Play Council:
- 45% of children said they were not allowed to play with water.
- 36% were not allowed to climb trees.
- 27% were not allowed to play on climbing equipment.
- 23% were not allowed to use bikes or skateboards.

Survey reported in the Guardian, *13 August 2002*

Parental anxiety may well be at the heart of the results of this survey – and such anxiety may well be legitimate. But if these are the same parents who allow their children to behave like adults in the way they dress, the kinds of magazines they read and the television programmes they allow them to watch, then we can see the mixed messages our children are receiving.

Make sure your group has a varied activity-based programme. Actively plan to give your children as many positive fun-filled experiences as possible.

Use as many games and practical activities as you can. Get hold of books of collaborative games – games that are non-competitive and will build self-esteem and a sense of team – and use them.

Seriously consider taking your group away for activity weekends and give them the opportunity to try some outdoor pursuits. This will build relationships, give the children the opportunity to try out some really fun stuff in a safe, supervised environment and build a real sense of self-esteem and achievement if they've never done these things before.

If you're a predominantly urban-based group, take your children away to an outdoor activity centre somewhere in the country. If you're a rural group, perhaps make links with a church in the centre of a town or city and take your group there.

Get hold of a copy of *Everyone's a Winner: Over 200 Co-operative Games and Activities for 7–13 Year-Olds* (Ruth Wills, SU 2002)

Reality Check

We've looked at what some of the 8–10s we interviewed are worried about, and we've seen how the media can fuel those fears. But what is the truth? What do the statistics tell us about children and the pressures they face? What are we really dealing with when we work with 8–10s from church and non-church backgrounds?

We do not have the space here to offer a full report on the complex culture our children grow up in. That is why the contact boxes for this chapter refer you to a wealth of other material we hope you will find helpful. What we have tried to do is pick up on some of the issues hinted at in our descriptions of Ben, Cherise and Alix, to explore the key facts related to them and to point you to the places where you can go for more detailed information.

The bare facts

The charity *Childline* lists the main problems dealt with by its helpline volunteers between April 2000 and March 2001:

- Bullying (17% of calls)
- Family relationships (14%)
- Physical abuse (11%)
- Sexual abuse (8%)
- Concern for others (8%)

Reported on the Childline *website,* August 2002

We can see elements of these and other pressures in our descriptions of the lives of Ben, Cherise and Alix. Let's explore some of the facts surrounding them.

Family relationships

In Alix's case, family relationships have been complicated by the divorce of her parents. For Cherise, living with her grandmother also involves a slightly chaotic relationship with her natural mother.

As teachers, we have often come across children whose behaviour shows some dramatic change for no apparent reason. A child may become suddenly withdrawn or unusually violent in their behaviour, and it is not until parents are asked to come into school to discuss the problem that a family break-up is identified as the trigger for the behaviour.

There are many organisations that have done helpful research both about the kinds of issues we deal with in this chapter, and other issues that matter to our age group. Often these organisations offer support and advice to children, their teachers and their parents.

Childline – a charity that offers children a confidential helpline. The website includes a great deal of helpful information about all kinds of issues facing children today, including abuse, eating disorders, stepfamilies, racism and bereavement.

www.childline.org.uk

The Joseph Rowntree Foundation – a research foundation whose website includes summaries of the wealth of research it has undertaken on all kinds of relevant issues.

www.jrf.org.uk

Kidscape – an organisation that works to provide support and advice to all those affected by bullying.

www.kidscape.org.uk

Bullying Online – a wealth of information about bullying, with advice for chidren, parents and teachers.

www.bullying.co.uk

The truth is that around one in four children will experience the separation of their parents while they are still at school. Others will live in families like Cherise, or in foster care. The family unit means many different things in our society.

The separation of parents means that children must cope with a whole series of changes that might include coming to terms with their parents' new partners, the introduction of stepbrothers and -sisters, living with one parent instead of two and dividing their time between two homes. Some children may have to move to a new area and change school. Alongside the emotional trauma of the initial separation can come a whole string of difficult changes. The routines and boundaries that give children their security can be turned upside down as they adjust to new living arrangements and step-parents who might have different rules and expectations.

Children's views about parental separation have been well documented by both Childline and the Joseph Rowntree Foundation:

- 25% of children with split parents said that no-one talked to them when the separation happened.
- Children caught up in conflict between parents and step-parents have more problems adjusting.
- Children value time to adjust and get to know their new stepfamily rather than being expected to be a 'perfect family' straight away.
- Children who have an active role in decisions about new living arrangements are more likely to be positive about their changed circumstances.

Children's Views of Their Changing Families, The Joseph Rowntree Foundation, 2001; Childline Information Sheet: 'Stepfamilies', 2002

Our response

However clear we are about the biblical ideals relating to marriage and families, we will be surrounded by children for whom these ideals have fallen short. Supporting them, through our attitudes towards them and our willingness to talk to them, will be a vital part of the work we do in building up trust between them and us. Knowing their circumstances helps us avoid embarrassment when we talk about home situations. Being inclusive in the things we say is important too. Cherise would feel instantly excluded if every time a note was given out at her mid-week club she was told to give it to her mum when she got home. If all the children were asked to get permission from a 'grown-up at home' for next week's swimming trip, Cherise would be included in the statement too. It's a simple detail, but an important one for children who are only too aware that their circumstances are different.

Aim to establish an atmosphere of stability and security within your group – something which the children may be missing out on at home. Talk with your group leaders and set appropriate but firm boundaries for behaviour when you and the children meet together. Be aware that these boundaries may be new to some children at first, but don't compromise.

Chapter Link

For more on effective discipline and setting boundaries, see Chapter Three.

Your hour or two of activity may be the only fixed point of stability in a child's week. In order to build secure and consistent relationships with your children over time, it will be important to have a committed team of leaders who are there fairly regularly. Having a leader's rota which is well-managed, where everyone is clear about boundaries, procedures etc and where there is opportunity for leaders to feed back between sessions, will be crucial.

Bullying

The name-calling Ben experiences as part of the school football team is something he can deal with himself for now. Other children do not have the same capacity for ignoring such behaviour. Cherise's difficulty in making friends is something many children face at some time or another; children are quick to spot others who are different and can be cruel in pointing it out. But when this kind of behaviour becomes targeted and consistent, the child on the receiving end is being bullied.

Bullying happens in all schools and all schools have a policy for dealing with it. Many organisations exist to support children who are victims and their parents, and to offer advice to schools on how to deal with bullying when it occurs. Children who are bullied may be on the receiving end of:
- name-calling
- taunts
- teasing
- threats
- physical assault.

In extreme cases children can be left frightened to go to school. But any child experiencing bullying is likely to feel, at least to some degree, that they have no friends and are not very likeable.

Our response

It has been estimated that approximately 15% of children are either bullied or guilty of bullying behaviour. Bullying is not exclusive to schools and could even happen within the group of 8–10s you are working with. Minor cases that are ignored can escalate into serious and systematic bullying, so it's important not just for schools but others working with children to have a policy for taking action when it occurs.

Poverty

Cherise laments her lack of pocket money, and we suspect she might have to be content with the basics for much of the time. Certainly we would not describe her as 'well-off'. She is not alone.

The findings of a survey commissioned by the Joseph Rowntree Foundation in 2000 suggest that two million children in Britain live in multiple deprivation and poverty. In the survey parents identified the following as necessities:

- adequate clothing
- a healthy diet
- items to support educational development
- an annual week's holiday away from home
- social activities.

However:

- 1 in 50 children go without new, properly fitted shoes, a warm waterproof coat and daily fresh fruit and vegetables.
- 18% go without two or more necessities.
- 34% go without at least one essential item.
- Around 9.5 million people cannot afford to keep their homes adequately heated or free of damp.

Children in homes where there is unemployment, a lone parent, or chronic illness or disability are most at risk.

Poverty and social exclusion in Britain, *Joseph Rowntree Foundation, 2000*

Think about the children in the group you work with. What do you know about their family situations? Are there parents who might be struggling, for whatever reason?

Are there others in your church who might be able to become involved in reaching out to and supporting these families?

Chapter Link

Also look at Chapter Three for ideas about positive discipline. This approach aims to create an atmosphere in which bullying is less likely to occur.

Our response

How do we respond to poverty like this? We need to engage with the culture we are part of, and if our church sits within a community where this kind of poverty exists, we cannot ignore it. Later on, in Chapters Six and Seven, we look at making an action plan for your work with 8–10s and then at different models of working. As you make your action plan, responding to the needs of the community will be an essential factor to consider. It may be these needs that provide the catalyst for a more innovative approach to the work you do. For example, a breakfast club might provide children with a healthy breakfast to start the day and an after-school club can provide a welcome refuge from a cold, damp house.

Child abuse

None of the three children we have introduced to you show any sign of coming from homes where abuse is happening, but there are children for whom it is a reality. In Chapter Seven we deal with the technicalities of Child Protection Policies and forms of abuse. The box opposite shows some figures regarding levels of child abuse in our society. Children who are hurt, neglected and used by adults or older children are victims of abuse. They can live under a veil of secrecy, frightened into keeping silent, or made to feel ashamed and responsible for what is happening.

Sometimes the result of abuse is physical injury and often there are serious and long-lasting emotional consequences. Childline's fact sheet on child abuse suggests that people who have been abused can grow up feeling:
- worthless
- unlovable
- betrayed
- powerless
- confused
- frightened
- mistrustful of others.

Our response

All advice on child abuse tells the victim to tell another adult they trust what is going on. This means that you could be the adult a child in your group chooses to tell. That's why your church must have a child protection policy, with clear lines of responsibility for dealing with such a disclosure. Above all, never promise a child that you will keep their secret in order to encourage them to tell you what is happening to them. It is a promise you cannot keep and will result in the breakdown of the trusting relationship they have with you.

It has been estimated that between 5% and 20% of women and between 2% and 7% of men have experienced sexual abuse. In the year 2000–2001:

- 7,154 girls talked to Childline about sexual abuse.
- 2,703 boys talked to Childline about sexual abuse.
- 13,285 children talked to Childline about physical abuse.
- 95% of children knew their abuser.

Childline Child Abuse Fact Sheet, 2002

The issue of child abuse can stir up strong emotions. Pause now and take time to be still before God and reflect on the words of Psalm 103:3–6,8:

> The LORD forgives our sins, heals us when we are sick,
> and protects us from death.
> His kindness and love are a crown on our heads.
> Each day that we live, he provides for our needs
> and gives us the strength of a young eagle.
>
> For all who are mistreated, the LORD brings justice ....
>
> ... The LORD is merciful! He is kind and patient,
> and his love never fails.

Is there hope?

It's a complex and at times depressing picture, isn't it? You will undoubtedly have identified a range of other concerns and pressures with your own group. Suddenly, working with this age group requires you to be a teacher, a social worker, a listening ear. Oh, and work your way through the minefield of what the church's response to all this should be! You need to be able to stick up for your 8–10s while others around you lament all that is happening, whilst not selling-out to their culture at the expense of biblical truth. And we wonder why recruiting leaders for this age group is a hard task!

But let's look at a picture of hope for a moment. Every summer thousands of children from church and non-church backgrounds go on Christian summer camps. What do they do there? Well, all kinds of things, but for a moment let's visit one in a field in Kent. On arriving at the site, we walk through a small wooded area. There are swings on some trees and a rope bridge between two others. A few children are playing here, chatting about the day ahead. Nearby is a stream. Here some leaders and children clad in wellington boots are in the stream, building a raft they will try to sail later. In the nearby log cabin a group of children are polishing pieces of wood to make a smooth surface for creating an ornament to take home. As they work, one of the leaders tells them stories. Throughout the day we will see these children again, sitting chatting with their friends as they sand down their piece of wood. A few other children are kicking a ball around in the open space. They sleep in tents at night and the highlight of the evening is the campfire and hot chocolate before bedtime.

We are watching children messing around in streams, playing in the woods and singing campfire songs. Suddenly we can see that deep down our 'tweenagers' are really still children. We need to be aware of their culture and ready to face up to the pressures of it with them. But we need to give them hope too, holding onto the knowledge that, even given all the statistics, they are survivors. And above all, we have the privilege of sharing Jesus Christ with them in a safe and loving environment. They need to hear from us a message that can transform their world:

> I have told you this, so that you might have peace in your hearts because of me. While you are in the world, you will have to suffer. But cheer up! I have defeated the world (John 16:33).

They won't hear it anywhere else.

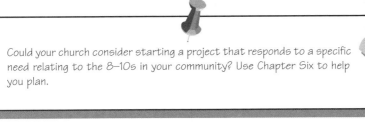

Could your church consider starting a project that responds to a specific need relating to the 8–10s in your community? Use Chapter Six to help you plan.

Chapter Three – A Question of Style

Think for a moment about a typical teaching session with the group of 8–10s you work with. What kinds of activities does it involve? The chances are, your list will include such things as storytelling, drama, games, craft and singing. Certainly these activities are the basics upon which the majority of published teaching programmes are built. But we need to be clear about why we do things this way, so that we don't fall into the trap of offering children lots of exciting activities with no clear purpose. So in this chapter we'll think a bit about how children learn, find out just what's happening in their schools and see how this can help us as we work with children in our churches.

What's happening in school?

Whilst we are not in the business of making our church's children's work identical to the school life the children encounter on a day-to-day basis, there is much we can learn from what happens in schools that will be useful to us. If you haven't been into a junior school within the last two or three years, make it a priority to do so as soon as possible. Not only will you have a better understanding of the world your 8–10s inhabit, you will pick up a host of useful ideas and strategies that you can apply when you teach these children in church.

Look at what might constitute a school day for Ben, Cherise or Alix. Let's unpack some of the jargon and begin to see what kinds of teaching and learning they encounter during the course of a typical day.

The Literacy Hour
Although the government originally suggested a fairly rigid format for the daily Literacy Hour, most schools have adapted it to their own particular circumstances. But in a typical session, you might see anything from children adapting a story into a radio play, to an investigation designed to explore a common spelling rule. They might be writing letters to the local council to complain about the volume of traffic outside their school, or designing a leaflet to advertise a local tourist attraction. They might work in groups, pairs or individually. The teacher may be working with a small group or with the whole class.

Numeracy
The start of the Numeracy Hour sees children working on their mental maths ability – securing knowledge of tables, basic number facts and operations so that they can apply these quickly in a range of contexts. The session moves into the introduction of the main task for the day and then the children work, again in groups, pairs or individually on a specific task, coming back together at the end of the session to summarise their learning.

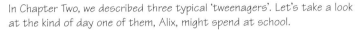

In Chapter Two, we described three typical 'tweenagers'. Let's take a look at the kind of day one of them, Alix, might spend at school.

Before school
Alix meets up with her friends in the playground. All have begged their parents to let them arrive a little early. They've just formed their own girl band and need to work on their dance routines.

Assembly
The headteacher talks about one of the school's Golden Rules: 'Do respect other people's property'. There have been some cases of stealing in one of the year groups and the headteacher uses the assembly to talk about why it's wrong to steal. He tells a story and then they have a short time to reflect on what he's said. They don't say a prayer, because there are people of several different faiths in the assembly.

Maths
Yesterday Alix's class did a traffic survey outside the school gates. They spend today entering the data into a computer program and talking about what they have found out. In their next IT lesson they'll get the same program to print off some graphs and charts to show the results of the survey.

Literacy
The reason for the traffic survey was to provide information for some letters to the council about the heavy volume of traffic outside the school. They spend Literacy preparing to write letters asking for a pelican crossing to be installed. First they look at other letters from the local newspaper written on similar issues. They use highlighter pens to pick out good words and phrases that they might be able to use in their own letters. They work in pairs and then report back to the rest of the class. The teacher records their suggestions on a flipchart, which she leaves up for the next day, when they will begin to draft their own letters.

Lunchtime
Alix has to eat her lunch quickly because she is her class's representative on the School Council and there is a meeting today. She's looking forward to discussing whether children should be allowed to have mobile phones in school. Her class have debated the issue and she wants to share their ideas with the rest of the council. The teachers have talked about it in their staff meeting too, and now they have to agree on a decision.

(Continued on page 49)

Children might conduct a traffic survey outside their school, calculate the cost of materials for improving the school playground or even work out the mathematical possibility of their favourite football team winning the Premiership!

ICT (Information and Communication Technology)

Rest assured, there are many 8–10s whose ICT knowledge will far outstrip yours! Most of them can do basic word processing and within strict guidelines they are able to carry out research and send messages using the Internet and email. But they might also set up a database to store information about a topic that interests them, enter their figures for materials for the school playground into a spreadsheet or edit a video of their school trip using digital technology.

Circle Time

Circle Time gives children the opportunity to work through issues that arise in their school – and sometimes their home – life. Skilfully managed, it is a powerful tool for resolving conflict and encouraging a class of children to support each other. As with all things, the exact format of a Circle Time will depend on specific circumstances, but typically there will be a warm-up activity designed to engender a sense of trust and co-operation followed by the opportunity to discuss issues relevant to the whole class or specific individuals. As a result Circle Time might become a forum for discussing bullying, friendship problems or school rules. The aim is to raise issues and involve the children in suggesting and working through possible solutions.

RE (Religious Education)

Many school inspection reports in recent years have commented on the lack of teaching of any form of spirituality in schools. Teachers who would not call themselves Christians often comment on the children's lack of knowledge of the Christmas and Easter narratives. Most children will leave junior school with a working knowledge of 2 or 3 religions (typically Christianity and then one or more of Islam, Judaism, Sikhism or Hinduism) but without having explored spirituality in any meaningful way. Many schools are not sure what their role should be in this area.

Inclusion

Inclusion is a relatively new term that many schools are grappling to get to grips with. The following definition is typical:

> [Inclusion] is about ensuring that opportunity and success are equally accessible to all members of the community; and that individuals and groups who may be marginalized, vulnerable or segregated do not experience disadvantage or discrimination in their education.
> *Bournemouth LEA Inclusion Strategy*

SEN (Special Educational Needs)

All schools must make provision for children at both ends of the special needs spectrum – those who find learning difficult and those who are classed as 'gifted and able'. In the past this has taken many forms, but with the current 'inclusion' agenda there is an increasing

(Continued from page 47)

Geography

Alix's class is learning about the local area, and this week they are looking at the school environment. In groups of three they are given a map of the school grounds and some photographs. They have to find out what part of the school the photo is of and mark it on their map. They have great fun exploring and when they get back to the classroom they add their photos to a big class display, and mark their position on an enlarged map. This display will be used to help visitors find their way round the school.

Circle Time

Straight after play, Alix and her classmates rearrange the tables in the classroom so there is a large space in the middle of the room. All the children bring their chairs and form a circle. The teacher joins them and Circle Time begins. Alix always sits with her friends for Circle Time, but this week the teacher makes them play a warm-up game that involves them all changing places. Then they return to the subject of stealing that they thought about in assembly this morning. Everyone is allowed to contribute and a beanbag is passed round to make sure everyone has their turn. You can only speak when you have the beanbag. They have a discussion about how having something stolen makes the victim feel. A couple of people in the class share their stories about when it happened to them. Then they all try to come up with solutions to help prevent the problem, before they end with another game.

After school

This is the day Alix has to be out of school quickly. She has to grab her swimming things and meet her mum at the gate. They whiz off to the local pool for her weekly swimming lesson. She asks mum to buy the local paper in the shop at the sports centre. Homework tonight is to look at the kinds of letters people write to their local paper. Next week her class are going to write letters to the paper themselves, drawing attention to the traffic problem.

Do you recognise this as the kind of school day you experienced? How can you find out what school life is like for your 8–10s?

expectation that the classroom curriculum will provide for every child, reducing the need for children to be taken out of class to be taught in small groups designed to address a particular need. This extends to children with challenging behaviour, for whom systems and strategies are devised that seek to keep such children within the classroom, so that they have the same opportunities as their peers to access the whole curriculum.

Other subjects

Alongside those we have already mentioned, Science, History, Geography, Music, PE and Design Technology are also on the primary curriculum. There is a huge body of knowledge from the reproduction of plants to the Roman Empire that children between the ages of 8 and 10 are expected to study. Whether or not such a curriculum really meets the needs of these children is open to question, but teachers know that the only way to make this knowledge accessible to the children is to plan learning experiences that explore key ideas through the use of role play, video, research projects, discussion and all kinds of practical tasks.

For almost every child between the ages of 8 and 10 that you encounter, these kinds of experiences will form part of their school day. It's important to notice that the approach to teaching and learning is a very active one. Children are used to talking about what they are doing and trying out new things through working together with other children and adults alike to make sense of their learning. It's worth noting too that when learning experiences are linked to things that matter to children (their own safety, their school playground) they are more likely to interest and engage them. More and more schools are setting up School Councils to actively involve children in decision making about their school. Children in the 8–10 age group are moving from dependence on adults to a degree of independence from them. Their learning needs to take account of this, allowing them to discuss and debate and make their own decisions.

How children learn

At any age, when we learn to do something new, it is likely that we will talk to others, try things out, and refine and review at each stage in the process. We do these things instinctively, and yet for the majority of us our learning in school was of a much more passive nature. If your memories of school evoke an image of a teacher at the front of the class explaining while you listened or took notes, it is likely that a visit to your local school would hold some surprises. That's because what we now know about how children learn demands a very different approach to how we teach them.

Have a look at the book below if you want to find out some practical ways of getting involved in your local school:

Generation to Generation – Building bridges between churches and schools, Fanfare For a New Generation/SU, 1999

Think of a new skill you have successfully learned recently. It could be anything from learning to use the Internet to salsa dancing!

How did you learn? Think about the factors that made your learning successful. Consider:

- Who supported you in your learning.
- How long it took you to learn.
- How you felt during the learning process
- How you overcame any problems you faced.
- Whether your learning involved listening, seeing, doing – and which of these helped you most.

Getting the right perspective

But before we delve into the theory, let's get our perspective right. Let's think about God's purpose in making us – and how he chooses to teach us.

When God said, '"Let us make man in our image"' (Genesis 1:26 NIV), he gave us a unique place in the created order. He assigned to us the capacity to be spiritual, intellectual and relational beings, with a moral capacity to discern right from wrong.

Through the work of his Holy Spirit, God wants us to become like Christ so that we reflect his glory (2 Corinthians 3:18). Through the work of the Spirit, God teaches and changes us to become more like him. This is important – God's purpose in teaching his people is about changing and moulding our characters. We may be concerned that our children don't know their Bibles, but by that we might simply mean that they can't list the books of the Bible in order, name all of Joseph's brothers and remember the exact words that God spoke to Jesus on his baptism. This is not God's perspective! He is far more interested in the kind of people we can become. So when he teaches us, he has his overall purposes in mind.

We know too that God made each of us to be unique, so it is probably safe to assume that we will not all learn in the same way. Reassuringly, you only need to start with the Bible and look at how God has taught his people down the years to see that what we now understand about how children (and adults for that matter!) learn is simply a reflection of the way God teaches us. The Bible itself is made up of different kinds of literature. Through its history books, its poetry, its prophecy and its letters we learn about God in a variety of ways. Jesus' style of teaching involved the use of parables and illustrations drawn from contexts relevant to his hearers. He often answered those who questioned him with a question of his own for them to consider. In other words, he involved his listeners in his teaching and expected them to actively engage with what they were hearing.

If we are serious about teaching children about God, we need to be clear about God's purposes. We also need to understand how they learn, and seek to teach them accordingly.

Redefining intelligence

God is concerned with every part of our beings – he even demands that we love him 'with all your heart, soul, mind, and strength' (Mark 12:30). Very often when we teach children we seek to engage their minds – but do we seek to engage their whole being?

How does God teach his people?

Ezekiel

Ezekiel 1–3

This passage records the detail of Ezekiel's vision.

- How does God get across the purpose of what Ezekiel must do?
- What kinds of images are used?
- Can you find examples of Ezekiel's need to use different senses as he makes sense of what God is saying to him?

The Ethiopian eunuch

Acts 8:26–40

Philip meets the Ethiopian man on the road from Jerusalem to Gaza.

- What information does the Ethiopian want to know?
- How does Philip explain it to him?
- What is the man's response?

James

James 1:19; 2:1–4; 4:11

Many people find James' letter helpful.

- Why might this be?
- Look at these passages and try to describe James' style.

Peter

Look at two of the key moments in Peter's life:

Matthew 14:22–32

- What does Peter learn about Jesus from this experience?

John 21:1–17

Peter learns about forgiveness, and is given his commission by Jesus.

- What can this become?
- What will Peter do with this new understanding?

Acts 2:14–47

- Reflect on Peter's teaching and lifestyle in response to all that Jesus has taught him.

Imagine for a moment that you have chosen to read aloud today's Bible story to your group. You give each of them a copy of the text. You read the first few verses and ask for volunteers to read several verses in turn. At the end of this you do a short quiz to see if they've remembered the key parts of the story. Let's see how three different children in your group might react to this:

Josh thrives on such an approach. He enjoys listening, particularly to the variety of voices provided by other children reading. He can answer nearly all the questions in the quiz.

Lucy complains that she can't remember much of the story. It was much better last week when there were pictures on the overhead projector to illustrate each part.

Jess can't even sit still while you read! Her concentration wanders and she can remember little about even the key facts of the story. Yet last week, when she helped you act out one of the parts in the story, she could answer pretty much all the questions in the quiz.

This is deliberately a little simplistic as we shall see, but it makes the point. Children will react to the same learning situation in different ways. Josh could be described as an **auditory** learner – a child who learns best through hearing. Lucy is a **visual** learner who learns best through seeing. Jess is a **kinaesthetic** learner and learns best through doing. Already we can see an important principle emerging – different children learn in different ways. The sad reality is that we often place value on particular ways of learning and disregard others. Thus the kinaesthetic learner might be perceived variously as 'lacking in concentration', 'a fidget' or just plain 'naughty'. But if we want to truly value all the children God gives us to work with, we may just need to redefine some of our thinking about exactly what we mean by such terms as 'clever' and 'well-behaved'.

The work of educationalist Howard Gardner challenges the traditional theory that intelligence is a capacity that can simply be measured by IQ tests. It is a theory that moves us towards a model of teaching and learning that begins to embrace the whole person.

Gardner identifies at least 7 different types of intelligence. His suggestion is that all of us possess all the different intelligences to different degrees and that, far from intelligence being a fixed commodity, it is possible, given a favourable learning environment, to strengthen all of them. The potential for their development, argues Gardner, will be affected by such external factors as personal choice, educational experiences, families and environment.

Visual, audio and kinaesthetic methods will appeal to different children in different ways. Consider some examples of each (below). Tick those you've tried – and resolve to try out some of those you haven't!

Visual
- Display key words around the room (names of places, people, themes to be explored through the Bible passage). ☐
- Use visuals and props to supplement the reading of stories (especially to help the children understand the context of Bible times). ☐
- Ask questions through visual recall ('What did it look like?) and visual imagination ('What would it look like?'). ☐

Audio
- Teach and practise good listening (remember to listen to the children as well as expecting them to listen to you!). ☐
- Use appropriate music to complement learning (even when the children are quietly writing or drawing, well-chosen music to evoke an atmosphere can help learning). ☐
- Use lots of singing, chanting and narrative verse. ☐
- Draw out the auditory references when telling stories ('It sounded like…', 'They heard…'). ☐

Kinaesthetic
- Use different areas of the room for different types of activity. ☐
- Act things out. ☐
- Use lots of toys and props to enhance storytelling. ☐
- Use physical associations such as movement, mime and gesture. ☐
- Learn by doing something. ☐
- Use role play. ☐
- Pretend to be people – walk and talk like them, mime their actions, imagine their feelings. ☐
- Ask questions through kinaesthetic recall ('What did it feel like..?', What would you be doing..?). ☐

Adapted from Alistair Smith and Nicola Call, *The APLS Approach – Accelerated Learning in Primary Schools*, Network Educational Press Ltd, 1999

Let's look briefly at the seven intelligences identified by Gardner, and the kinds of people who might display these characteristics:

- Linguistic – the ability to communicate and make sense of the world through language (poets and writers).
- Musical – the ability to perform, compose and appreciate music, alongside a heightened response to intonation and rhythm of voice (composers).
- Logical-mathematical – the ability to use and appreciate abstract concepts and offer logical analysis of problems (scientists, mathematicians, philosophers).
- Spatial – the ability to perceive and transform visual or spatial information (architects and engineers).
- Bodily-kinaesthetic – the ability to use all or part of the body to create products and solve problems (athletes, surgeons, craftspeople).
- Interpersonal – the ability to understand other people and to work effectively with them.
- Intrapersonal – the ability to be self-aware – to know one's own emotions, desires and fears, strengths and weaknesses, and react appropriately to them.

The final two intelligences are harder to spot amongst our 8–10s. They are about an awareness of ourselves and others, and this is an area where much development takes place within our age group. Developing them will build the kind of understanding of themselves and others that will help them to form effective relationships.

These are simply snapshots of the different intelligences, but it is likely that, even from these basic descriptions, you can begin to identify where your strengths are. You may also be able to identify the strengths of some of the children in the group you work with. What we are beginning to see is that our group will be made up of children whose intelligence can be defined in different ways. This means that the ways in which they learn will be different – and somehow we need to address this! If we adopt one dominant teaching style (probably the one that best reflects how we ourselves learn) then we can be sure that a significant proportion of the children we teach will not be learning effectively.

This presents a somewhat new perspective on the children in our group who frustrate us and who we find hard to teach. There will always be children who cause us specific problems and for who discipline is an issue, and we shall return to this later. But consider how hard it must be for someone whose bodily-kinaesthetic intelligence is well defined to be taught by someone whose preferred style of delivery involves the use of lots of reading and writing activities.

Can you name any children in your group who possess these characteristics? What implications does this have for your response to them?

Linguistic – Is there a child in your group who loves to tell jokes and stories?

Musical – Is there a child who drives you mad by tapping rhythms with their pencil, or being distracted by the birds singing outside?

Logical-mathematical – This is the child who can present you with the mathematical possibilities related to their favourite team winning the Premiership!

Spatial – The child who draws intricate patterns on a blank sheet of paper as you carefully explain what you want them to do.

Bodily-kinaesthetic – These are the children who want to act out the story, build models, put together a dance routine – anything rather than sit still!

Suddenly, an inability to sit still becomes an expression of a desire to get on with learning in a more active way. If we simply assume it is a lack of discipline and thus make clear our dissatisfaction, the child will, whether consciously or subconsciously, infer that such a learning preference is not valued. Quite apart from the fact that such a message can only have a detrimental effect on a child's inclination to learn, it is not a message we want to present to children who we believe are unique and special in God's eyes.

Other factors

How long can you concentrate for? The average concentration span of an adult is something in the region of 20 minutes. But what about our 8–10s? It is suggested that their average concentration span is approximately equal to their chronological age in minutes plus two minutes (Mike Hughes, *Closing the Learning Gap*, 1999). In other words, an 8-year-old in your group is likely to have a maximum attention span of ten minutes!

This has obvious implications for the kinds of sessions we plan for our groups of 8–10s. Their learning is likely to be more effective if we divide our session into a series of activities. But what else do we know about how children learn that can inform the kinds of activities we plan?

Firstly, some basic understanding of how the brain works can help. The left side of the brain is the logical part. It is the side of the brain we use when we read, write and listen to process the information we receive. The right-hand side is more comfortable with the random and intuitive. It responds to things such as colour, pictures and music. What is important to remember is that these two sides of the brain do not work in isolation – the brain functions at its best when both sides are fully engaged. 'Not only is the brain able to cope with multi-sensory simultaneous input, it actually prefers it!' (Mike Hughes, *Closing the Learning Gap*).

Secondly, the brain is more likely to remember the *context* of a learning experience than the *content*. This is the reason why inviting children to participate in a real baptism service will have a far greater impact than inviting the minister to come and talk to them about what happens. Participation makes the learning context more dramatic and engages the emotions. It places learning in a memorable context and makes it easier to recall at a later date.

The context of a teaching and learning experience is very important. So is the amount of active involvement in the learning process. Write down three ways you will adapt your next teaching session as you begin to address some of these issues.

Chinese proverb:
Telling is not teaching
Listening is not learning
Reading is not studying
You learn by doing.

We remember:
10% of what we read
50% of what we see
60% of what we say
and
90% of what we do!

Have you ever had one of those Sundays when you overslept, the children first refused to get dressed and then argued all the way in the car, and then, when you finally arrived at church five minutes after the start of the service you were greeted by a minister just in the middle of delivering a brief lecture on the frustrations of a congregation who never arrive on time? It's safe to say that when the sermon begins you are unlikely to be in the frame of mind to take it in!

And this is an important consideration when it comes to how children learn too. Learning should be a challenging activity, but we respond best to a challenge when we feel safe and relaxed in our environment. This means that the layout of the furniture in a room, the displays on the wall and even something as simple as whether we greet the children with a smile when they arrive all have an important part to play in creating the right conditions for learning.

It's also important that we allow the children some control over what happens in a session. The temptation is to have a session so tightly planned that the children have no freedom at all. In fact, it is possible to plan opportunities into a session that allow the children enough freedom to feel that they have some choice and independence. Something as simple as being allowed to choose where to sit, or deciding whether to use crayons or felt tips for a particular activity can make a difference.

The beginning of a learning experience is crucial for a child. Mike Hughes suggests in *Closing the Learning Gap* that the key learning point should preferably be introduced within the first 60 seconds of a lesson, and certainly within the first five minutes. The start should always be purposeful and if this purpose can be provided by an imaginative and unexpected activity, a healthy context for learning will be established. It's worth remembering that if a session is divided up into a series of activities in order to sustain concentration, then each activity will have its own beginning. This means there is an opportunity for a series of engaging moments throughout the lesson that will maintain momentum.

Teaching children in church

Theory is great, isn't it? It always sounds good, but in practice it's never quite so straightforward! You may well be nodding your head vigorously in agreement with all that we have said about styles of learning, whilst at the same time wondering if actually what we're trying to suggest is that you suddenly change everything you've ever done, reinventing the wheel with a whole host of new kinds of activities.

Chapter Link

We think more about the learning environment in Chapter seven.

Find a plan for a teaching session you have used/plan to use.

- Does it follow the learning cycle (see page 62)?
- Is there a range of activities to address the needs of different learning styles?
- If not, how might you adapt the session to meet these needs?

There is some quite readable material available on the issues we've discussed relating to how children learn. Try:

Mike Hughes, *Closing the Learning Gap*, Network Educational Press Ltd, 1999

Alistair Smith and Nicola Call, *The ALPS Approach — Accelerated Learning in Primary Schools*, Network Educational Press, 1999

Marlene LeFever, *Learning Styles — Reaching Everyone God Gave You to Teach*, Kingsway, 1998

Chapter Link

Look at Chapter Five for lots more ideas on session planning and activities.

Be reassured! The drama, the games, the quizzes, the craft that you do each week will already be addressing many of the children's learning preferences. If you use a published programme, the reason such activities are included is precisely because those writing the material have an understanding of how children learn.

So, based on what we've discovered so far, we want to offer children learning opportunities that are meaningful and allow them the opportunity to become actively involved in the learning process. But we know too that the children we encounter will learn best in a variety of ways. How on earth do we translate this thinking into a manageable approach to teaching?

Learning styles in church

The work of Marlene LeFever has done a great deal to examine styles of learning and relate them to a Christian perspective. She accepts the challenge an understanding of how people learn presents:

> Learning styles will make our jobs as Christian educators more difficult. No longer can we teach the way we like to learn and assume everyone will learn. No longer can we make an easy judgement about who's clever and who's not. Learning styles force us to rethink how we teach and adjust to the way God made people – not the way we used to think he made them, or even the way we wish he'd made them.
> *Marlene LeFever*, Learning Styles, *Kingsway, 1998*

LeFever proposes a learning cycle to provide a lesson structure that naturally addresses the needs of a range of types of learner. As we work through it in the light of all that we have discovered during the course of this chapter, we can see that it gives a helpful framework for learning.

Stage 1

This is the beginning of the lesson, and is crucial in establishing a purpose for learning. It is also the opportunity to relate the subject to the children's existing knowledge. It provides the opportunity to listen and share ideas based on personal experience and thus provides a context for subsequent learning.

This is where the key teaching point will be introduced and imaginations will be engaged. It is the time to introduce the theme and relate it to the children's own experience.

Let's use the story of Daniel to work out how we might apply the learning cycle in practice. Read Daniel 6. Study the Bible passage, look at the kinds of activities suggested – and maybe add some ideas of your own!

Stage 1 – Introduce the theme: TRUST
You could:
- Play a trust game – perhaps a blindfolded obstacle course, where one child guides another.
- Lead a discussion about the kinds of people we trust.
- Get the children to role-play situations in which one person needs to trust another.

Stage 2 – Add new information: WHAT DOES THE BIBLE HAVE TO SAY?
Tell the story from Daniel 6. You could:
- Read the story from a suitable version, then split it into smaller sections and give pairs or small groups some questions to explore and report back.
- Give groups a different part of the passage to act out.
- Prepare a script of the story for the children to read aloud.

When the group has got to grips with the passage, challenge them to go through it again, and highlight the places where Daniel shows that he trusts God.

Stage 3 – Applying the knowledge: WHAT DOES THIS MEAN FOR ME?
You could:
- Role-play common situations when it's hard to trust God. How might they handle these?
- Discuss times when they are under pressure to do things they know wouldn't please God. Brainstorm ways of responding that rely on trusting God.
- Find a suitable TV programme that shows a child struggling with the pressure of peers to do something they don't want to do. How might trusting in God make a difference here?

Stage 4 – Putting it into action: WHAT SHALL I DO NOW?
Ask the children to think of one thing they will do this week to help them trust God more. You could:
- Get them to choose a verse from Daniel 6 that reminds them to trust God. Write it out, decorate it and use it to help them pray during the week.
- Get them to share the areas of their life where they want to trust God to help them. Pray together in the group and promise to pray for each other during the week.
- Make a prayer board. Each child draws or writes about a situation in which they need to trust God to help them. Use their writings and drawings to make a prayer collage.

Beware: the children might have other ideas! Encourage them to put the teaching into practice in a way that is suitable for them!

Suppose you are looking at the theme of trust. For those learners for whom feelings and the sharing of ideas is important, the use of activities such as role play in the first stage of the learning cycle will help to engage them with the subject under discussion. They will enjoy working with others to explore situations in the context of their own lives where trust is involved. Such role play can help lead them to the point where they see the importance of being able to trust others in certain situations. The concept of trusting Jesus then becomes relevant for them – they have a purpose for wanting to discover more.

Stage 2

As the session moves on, the teacher seeks to build on existing experience and knowledge by adding new facts and information to move the group on in their understanding. So, the theme that has so far been explored from the viewpoint of the children can now be explored from a biblical perspective. What does the Bible have to say on the subject? Some children will be excited by the challenge of finding out new information. These are the children who enjoy delving into the Bible to see what it has to say and sharing what they have found with others.

Stage 3

Armed with the necessary facts, the next stage of the learning cycle plays to the strengths of those children who want to go on and use the information they have gained. It is not enough simply to know it; they want to apply their knowledge, using it in real contexts. This means that the whole group can be encouraged to grapple with the issues and see how they might be applied in real and contemporary contexts.

Returning to the theme of trust, these learners will want to see how the biblical concept can be applied. They want to know whether it 'works' in the context of their own lives. It will not be enough to be told that Jesus can be trusted. Give them the opportunity to think about a situation in which they might need to trust Jesus and hand the problem over to them. What might happen if they did trust Jesus in this situation? What if they didn't?

Stage 4

This is the stage when the more creative and dynamic learners come to the fore. They 'want to enlarge what they have learned, adding creative ideas and perhaps teaching what they have learned to others'. (Marlene LeFever, *Learning Styles*, p40) These children might provide the idea that excites the whole group to put into action what they have learned in a way that neither the leaders nor the rest of the group had considered. This kind of spontaneity cannot be planned for, but might well be the very thing that the children will always remember.

Think of an incident where there was a discipline issue with one or more of the children in your group? What went wrong? How did you handle it? How did the child(ren) respond? Have you ever thought about some of the reasons behind the problem behaviour?

Boredom
- Because they don't like the activity.
- Because it goes on too long.
- Because there is a gap with nothing to do.
- Because things are badly planned (attention, cooperation, enthusiasm is lost).

Insecurity
- Because of their personal needs.
- Because of disorganisation in the group making them uncomfortable and insecure.
- Because of uncertainty about their place or status in the group.

Differing standards
- Because it is acceptable at home.
- Because they are so involved they are not thinking.
- Because it is 'their' club so it should be as they want it.
- Because 'they' is seen to be them alone – not the majority.

High spirits not channelled
- Because of inappropriate activities.
- Because of the wrong mix of activities.
- Because of the lack of space, facilities, supervision.

Resentment
- Because they are there through parental pressure, not choice.
- Because they don't like or respect the leaders.
- Because they are having an 'off day'.

Attention seeking
- Because of their personal needs.
- Because they are being ignored by leaders (watch out for leaders talking to each other and not to the kids).

And what about…
- Fear of a particular activity?
- Fear of other people?
- Testing boundaries?

This learning cycle is a helpful approach because it can provide a clear structure for what we are doing, ensuring that the activities we plan really do meet the needs of different learners. No one child will find all parts of the session equally accessible, but they should actively be able to connect with at least part of what takes place. How they deal with the rest of the session will depend on their relationship with the other children in the group. If these relationships are positive, the children will work together to support one another in all parts of the session, drawing on one another's strengths and compensating for weaknesses.

Of course, we do not live in an ideal world. Not all schools and teachers consistently teach in ways that genuinely engage all kinds of learners. Sometimes there remains an underlying assumption that these 'new' methods are all very well, but the old traditional ways remain the best. There are children in schools, and thus quite probably in your group, who are being let down by a system that does not genuinely value their learning needs. There are others who, for whatever reason, have lives outside of school that hinder their ability to learn in school. Sometimes the reaction to this is to be disruptive.

What about discipline?

However, we would not want to suggest that adopting an approach to teaching and learning that addresses all that we know about how children learn will eliminate all discipline problems. That would be some claim! What about the children who cause problems regardless of the activities we offer? Whilst we may want to look a little deeper to understand what causes them to behave the way they do, in the short term maintaining effective discipline is important for the good of the group as a whole. So how do we do it?

Positive behaviour policies exist in every school. They work on the common sense principle that children respond best when they are rewarded for positive behaviour rather than just punished for bad. This is surely something we would want to endorse in our work with children. Positive behaviour policies start from the assumption that all children should be valued. In sharing the Christian faith with them, we want them to see that they are valued by God, even though they do wrong things. Using positive behaviour strategies can help us to present this message effectively.

Specific responses to specific problems:

'I want to be noticed'
- Make sure all the kids get group time with a leader who listens to them to try and avoid the need for attention-seeking; give individual time if possible.
- Promise to talk to them at a suitable time and do so.
- Try to find out the reason for the attention-seeking: insecurity? Low self-esteem? Problems at home? No friends? Then try to address the problem (eg praise for a task well done, a home visit, link them into a friendly peer group).

'I don't want to be here'
- Talk to them about what they would rather be doing – can you offer this? Do you know someone who can?
- Help them to think about the effect of their attitude on others.
- Are they worried about an activity? – encourage them to help you 'lead' in some way, eg keep score or simply watch.
- Talk sensitively to the parents/guardians if the kids are really unhappy about being involved or being present – why are they coming/sent?
- If they are being difficult, remind them of the acceptable boundaries.

'I want to carry on'
- Tell them there will be some time later to finish what they are doing – and plan it in.
- Enthuse about what is to happen next and how they are needed to be a part of it.
- If they are still reluctant, see if they have a problem with the next activity – it may be best to let them sit out of it.
- If they won't go home, talk to them about it and find out why – don't just throw them out.

'It's boring'
- Explain why you're doing the activity.
- Encourage them to see the point of it, get involved, go off at a tangent if that will keep them interested.
- Promise them something different later, or next time – and do it!
- Use their ideas, eg if they make paper airplanes out of worksheets, have a paper airplane competition next time!

(Continued on page 69)

There are two key elements that make a positive behaviour strategy work.

1 Boundaries

The first is the setting of clear boundaries. If we want to promote acceptable behaviour, the children need to know what is and isn't okay. Schools often begin the academic year by involving the children in the drawing up of class 'Golden Rules'. Their language is always positive (for example, 'Do listen to others' rather than 'Do not interrupt') and the aim is to set clear guidelines for behaviour. It wouldn't hurt to do a similar exercise with the group you work with. All of us are more likely to stick to rules that we have some ownership of. If your children have agreed to the rules from the outset, it is easier to challenge them when they choose to deviate from them! (But beware – it's also easier for them to challenge you if you don't stick to the rules!)

With children at the older end of our age group, we can begin to talk about how their meeting is different from school and what makes it feel different. We can decide whether some rules can be relaxed and the implications this will have on each person. The children can consider which rules might need to stay the same and the reasons for this. Again, we are simply involving the children in setting boundaries and helping them to see the importance of the group being a nice place to be.

Once clear boundaries have been set, the children need to see a positive response when they act within them, not just a negative response when they step outside them. Again you can involve the children in setting up a reward system; they will have experience of all sorts of systems in the schools they attend. Exactly what system you employ is less important than the fact that you have a system at all. It means that the focus of all that you do is on encouraging good behaviour rather than simply trying to prevent bad. You can move on from here to asking the children what they think should happen if someone breaks the rules. Children are generally harsher in their suggestions for sanctions than we would be! We need to be clear with them that the overall aim is to keep a good atmosphere in the group rather than to impose severe punishments on others!

2 Relationships

If the children see that overall your intention is to be positive and encouraging in your dealings with them, they will begin to trust you and believe that you value them. This is the basis for the second important factor in developing a positive approach to managing behaviour – what in schools is called the pupil/teacher relationship.

(Continued from page 67)

'I've nothing to do'
- Have extra activities for them – planned in advance.
- Spend time chatting with them.
- Aim your timing of activities (eg craft) to meet those working at a medium pace – have fillers for the faster kids and additional time (or arrange to take things home) for the slower kids.

'I want to do this'
- Challenge them to think of others and not just of their own rights – encourage a sense of responsibility and sharing: 'It's our club…'
- Meet them halfway, eg if some of the group want to play football and you've planned uni-hoc, explain why their attitude is unhelpful (everyone's wishes count, not just those of a few) and promise to play football later/next time.
- You may need to use formal discipline strategies here.

(The material on this page and pages 65 and 67 is taken from *Stop it or else!* by Kathryn Burgin, Scripture Union)

On reflection, are there occasions in your group when unacceptable behaviour might be the result of one of the reasons identified here?

Would you handle things differently another time?

When we work with children in our churches our relationship with them is crucial. They must see Jesus in us, and yet see our human weakness too. Whether we like it or not, we become at least to some extent role models for the children we work with. How we deal with them and their behaviour will have an effect on how they deal with others.

What we have on our side with this age group is their developing ability to step outside of a situation and see someone else's point of view. This means that we can ask them to reflect on the impact of their behaviour on others, and expect them to be able to display at least a degree of empathy in their response.

How does this work out in practice? What kinds of behaviour strategies can we use to develop and maintain positive relationships with the children we work with? It helps if we think about this from the point of view of our reaction to the behaviour and then our response to it.

It is easy to take a child's bad behaviour personally, to believe they are specifically getting at us. This is rarely the case and reacting in this way can lead to an almost hysterical response on our part. Take a child who responds rudely when you ask them to stop talking during an explanation of an activity. How often are we tempted to say something like, 'I give up my time to come here and do this club, and this is how you behave! I can't believe you could be so ungrateful!'

Sadly, such a response is likely to inflame the situation further, and lead to a confrontation. Once this point is reached, someone has to back down, and someone else has to 'win'. The result is a damaged relationship.

How might the situation be different if your initial reaction is to calmly but firmly impose a sanction that the child is familiar with (perhaps asking them to move away from the group whilst you complete your explanation)? In this scenario, the initial disruption is dealt with and the rest of the children can begin the task. None of the children have to witness the kind of unwelcome reaction we saw above. You still need to deal with the behaviour itself, but this can now be done in a calm one-to-one setting where you restate set boundaries and ask the child to consider the impact of their behaviour both on you and the rest of the group. How much more likely you are to maintain a positive relationship with the child themselves, as well as a positive atmosphere within the group as a whole.

Why discipline? What does the Bible have to say?

Proverbs 3:11,12 and 13:24
- What motivates discipline? (See also Hebrews 12:5,6)

Proverbs 29:17
- What is the result of effective discipline? (See also Hebrews 12:5,10,11)

The most important principle here, and something we must always be clear about with the children, is that it is the behaviour and not the child that we do not like. In our dealings with children who cause us problems we must somehow help them to see that we still value them as a person, that in fact it is because we care about how they feel that we want to address the problem with them. This is how God deals with his children when we get things wrong, and the children must see this in us.

Considering how God deals with his children is important because it gives us a clear mandate for using discipline with the children we work with. Sometimes we try to hard not to make the group too much like school, and in trying to develop a good relationship with the children we mistakenly assume that we should give the children a free rein in terms of behaviour. Yet if we have children of our own we know that they need discipline to make sense of their world. They need to know what is okay and what isn't, and the children we work with at church need to know the same. Using positive discipline strategies gives us an approach that maintains discipline without damaging relationships.

Involving parents

Working with children in our churches is different from working with them in schools. The children don't have to be there, their parents can choose whether or not to send them, and we can even choose whether or not we want to teach them! This means that relationships with parents are going to be an important factor in determining whether the models of discipline we adopt are successful. Not all parents will share our views on positive discipline – and some parents may be struggling to discipline their children themselves.

There will be children who step out of line from time to time and often an informal chat with the parent can address the problem successfully. But if the disruption continues or if there is a child with a particular behavioural problem within the group more serious action may be necessary. In such cases there needs to be a clear procedure that can be followed to address the problem. If you have someone who has general oversight of all the youth and children's work in your church, it's worth working with them to get such a procedure in place. If this is not the case, then involving the church leadership is important. Everyone needs to know what happens if there is a discipline issue with a particular child.

Involving parents isn't just about telling them if their child is misbehaving. Letting them know about the good things that happen in your group is equally important. Below are some suggestions for involving parents. You may want to add one or two of your own. Then resolve to try one or more of them out over the coming term!

- Make a display of the work you have done on a particular theme. Get the children to give their parents a 'guided tour' of the display.

- Send home a short summary of the session and suggest a follow-up activity that could be done at home.

- Talk to the parents of one or two of your group each week during coffee after the service. Tell them one positive thing their child has contributed to the group that week.

- Invite the children and their parents to stay after the session once a term for a picnic lunch. When everyone has eaten, have a short, child-friendly time of prayer for the group.

Every situation will be different, but there are some principles worth bearing in mind if you want to maintain both effective discipline and good relationships with parents:

- Establish shared expectations. If you have agreed a set of rules with your group, let the parents know what they are.
- Communicate with parents as much as possible if there is a discipline issue involving their child. Whilst we need to avoid over-reacting by informing parents of every minor misdemeanour, most parents don't want to hear about a problem for the first time when it has reached the stage of being a major issue.
- As with the child themselves, be clear with parents that it is the behaviour and not their child that you don't like. Ask them what they do at home to try to encourage good behaviour and agree on some strategies to try.
- Be aware that children who find it hard to behave may also be causing their parents a good deal of trouble. Be prepared to involve others in your church who might be able to offer support to the parents too.
- Be prepared to invest time in the children who find behaviour difficult. Offering some one-to-one support to a particular child may enable them to stay in the group, whilst minimising their disruptive influence on everyone else.

Remember that the children you work with spend a great deal more time at home than they do with you. Investing time in building good relationships with their parents can only have a positive impact on the work you are trying to do.

God's children

All that we have considered in this chapter should help us to value the children God has given us to work with and find ways of meeting their unique and individual needs. But this is no easy task, however much we understand about them! Thankfully God has not left us on our own to do the job. This is why the most valuable thing you can do for each and every child in your group is to pray for them. You can begin to know them better as you develop a relationship with them. God knows them completely.

Chapter Four – Face to Face

It is temptingly easy to look back at your own childhood through rose-coloured spectacles, and think that back then, life was simpler, the world was a kinder place and everyone had more fun. The current craze for 'School Disco' nights at clubs, or the rash of *I Love 1975* programmes on TV show us how much we love to relive our past. But today's children don't need us to relive our past – they need us to live their present. If we are to work effectively with 8, 9 or 10-year-old children, we need to forget some of our cherished but dated ideas of what children *should be* like, and work hard to understand what they *are* like.

And it isn't all doom and gloom! Some of the changes in our culture provide us with wonderful opportunities to try new things and to think creatively. We must never forget that God has often gone before us, and will work miracles in seemingly impossible circumstances. To encourage you, we've devoted this chapter to real-life interviews with three 21st century children. Zoe, Lisa and Sam all live in the same town, but have quite different backgrounds. They share with us what they like doing, what worries them and what they think about God. Their stories provide living illustrations of some of the things we have thought about in the first three chapters, and pose some challenging questions as we go on to consider how the church responds to the children of today.

Case Study: Zoe and Lisa

We met Zoe and Lisa in Zoe's house one morning in the school holidays. Zoe and Lisa are both 10, although Zoe made sure we knew that she would be 11 in January and Lisa had only been 10 in July. Even at this age, the girls could work out their ages to the nearest quarter of a year, and were quite clear who was the oldest! Lisa's mum dropped her off at Zoe's house, and came in for a quick chat with Zoe's mum. Before children go off to secondary school, parents are still very involved with their children's friends, will often have built up good friendships themselves with the other parents, and have developed a good network of support, mutual lift-sharing, etc.

Lisa led the way up to Zoe's room. She was playing an S Club CD quite loudly, but fortunately had her own doorbell fixed up outside which Lisa rang to get her attention. Her room is small, but tidy. She informed us that she had rearranged it that morning. She had painted it herself the previous year, and obviously valued having control over her own space. Both girls talked about their rooms as a haven, somewhere where they could be themselves, take friends, play music and occasionally go for a sulk or to cry.

We asked the girls how they became friends.

Lisa: I don't know! In Reception we weren't in the same class, but in Year One we were. Now we're best friends.

Zoe: And we also met each other by going to dancing and netball. I met Lisa in Year One. We played with each other, we played at ponies. All our friends, we go round in like a gang. We're practically all so close, that we hardly ever have an argument, or only for stupid reasons.

Q: How many are in your gang?

Lisa: Six

Zoe: Five or six.

Q: Is there one person who's sort of sometimes in and sometimes out?

Zoe: Yeah, there is one person, she normally plays with boys, or these two girls, they're both like tomboys.

Q: Are all your friends from school, or have you got other friends?

Lisa: Quite a few.

Zoe: I've got loads – some from church, some from down the road, some from all my other clubs. Oh, and we've got this gang – loads and loads of people who live round this area. We have gang meetings – oh, and Lisa's in it as well.

Lisa: Yes, normally we go out on Tuesdays and Thursdays.

Zoe: And we go out to places like Beacon Hill and the beach.

All the places the girls mentioned going to with their gang were several miles away. This gang was made up of the children of their parents' friends, who were all of a similar age and obviously got on well. The girls both have several sets of friends for different circumstances. They are starting to make friends independently, at school and clubs, but are also still very involved with their parent's friends' families. Lisa had just returned from a holiday her family shared with two other families.

Q: *Have you got any friends that are boys, or are all of your friends girls?*

Zoe: I've got lots of friends out of school who are boys, and I've got a boyfriend out of school, but mostly all the boys at school are geeks.

Q: *Do you ever play with any of the boys?*

Zoe: We play with Robert and Joe quite a lot, and they're quite nice…

Both girls look at each other and giggle. We probe a bit further about their relationship with the boys.

Lisa: Well, I like Joe and Joe likes me. If they are playing a game, sometimes we go and join in, if there's nothing to play. It's quite good because if you score a goal or catch the ball they go, 'Yeah, Lisa!'

Q: *Zoe, can I ask you about your boyfriend, or is it really secret?*

Zoe: No, I met him on holiday, organised by the youth club at church.

The girls are obviously starting to be interested in boys. They giggle a lot, and look away, as they both talk about their boyfriends.

Q: *Have you seen him since the holiday?*

Zoe: Yeah, lots. At the beach, the shops…

Q: *Would you phone him up and go round to his house, like you might Lisa's?*

Zoe: No, I wouldn't go round to his house, but I would phone him up and ask if he wants to come down the park with me, or something like that.

The girls seem to be firmly in charge of these relationships. They talk about a friend of theirs who dumped a boyfriend, and agree that it is normally the girl who first approaches a boy rather than the other way round.

To find out what things they enjoyed doing, the girls imagined they had £10 to spend – what would they do?

Zoe: Spend it!

Lisa: Cool!

Zoe: I'd probably go down to the shops with my friends.

Q: *What would you spend it on?*

Zoe: Clothes, whatever.

Lisa: If it was a cheque, then I'd put it in the bank. If I'm saving up for something, I'd save it. Normally, I'd go down the shops and buy sweets or something.

Q: Which shops would you go to, if you were going to spend your £10?

Lisa: I'd go to New Look or Tammy…

Zoe: Clothes shops.

Q: How do you decide what to buy?

Zoe: How much it is, or if it suits you, or if it's nice, if it's fashionable.

Q: How do you know whether it's fashionable or not?

Lisa: I ask my friends. My friend has got two older sisters, so she knows what's fashionable. I asked her when it was my birthday and I wanted some clothes. Sometimes I know what's fashionable… I like collecting Beanie Kids and Beanie Babies. I bought two of them last week on holiday.

Q: Do you buy music as well?

Zoe: Yes, CDs.

Lisa: I get my mum to buy them, because they're expensive.

Zoe: I got the Blue album for my birthday. I've got S Club 7, Liberty X. I get lots of singles, because they're cheap.

By the age of 10, the girls are a mixture of children who buy sweets, play with their friends and come across as unsophisticated, blended with the 'tweenager' beloved by advertisers who is interested in fashion, pop music and boys. The most encouraging evidence of growing up was their independence, their ability to decide for themselves whether to follow a trend or not, the responsibility they showed towards their possessions and their friends. These two girls seem unaffected by, though not unaware of, the problems of our society.

Lisa: Sometimes I worry that if I make some new friends and they smoke, they'll ask me if I want to smoke too. If I try one, then if I like it I'll keep doing it. I don't want to do that.

Zoe: These girls down the road, they smoke, they take drugs, one of them's pregnant… Well, quite a few of them are pregnant. There's a whole road of them.

Q: How do you know that they take drugs?

Zoe: On Friday nights, when I have a friend to sleep over, we look out from the attic and see them really clearly.

Lisa: Sometimes you can't get to sleep because they all shout and make loads of noise.

Zoe: You can hear them all swearing when you are in the shower. Loads of people in this road, they're either really sad, so they swear, or just not nice at all.

Q: Why do you think they take drugs and smoke?

Zoe: To be popular.

Q: Where do you think they get drugs from?

Zoe: From the shop down the road.

Q: Has anyone ever offered you drugs?

Zoe: No, because we only go down there during the day. And even if they are there, they're normally talking in a group.

Zoe has mentioned the youth club at her local church. Both of her parents are Christians, with her mum particularly involved in the life of the church. Lisa's parents don't go to church, but Lisa has been a few times with Zoe.

Q: Do you go to church?

Zoe: Yes

Lisa: Normally I don't, but if I go round Zoe's, I normally go to her church.

Q: What do your family think about going to church?

Lisa: We normally don't, but I don't know why. I like going to Zoe's church, it's fun.

Q: Have you ever talked to your mum and dad about going to church or if they believe in God?

Lisa: Not really.

Q: What about you, Zoe? Do you talk to your mum and dad about God?

Zoe: No… I read my Bible every day. It's really fun.

Q: Did anyone suggest to you that was a good idea, or was it just something you decided to do?

Zoe: It's just something I do.

Q: Does your mum check up on you?

Zoe: Yes… Sometimes we do my Bible notes together. I'm not sure what she'd say if I didn't want to do it. And I have five minutes of praying to Jesus before I go to sleep…

Q: Have you always prayed, since you were little?

Zoe: Yes, I've been a Christian since I was 2.

Q: What about you, Lisa, would you say you are a Christian, or are you not sure?

Lisa: Yes, I'm a Christian. I got christened when I was about 4 months old. I believe in God and Jesus…

Zoe: The Holy Spirit?

Lisa: Mmmm. Most people in my school don't believe in things like Father Christmas and the Tooth Fairy, but I still believe in them.

Q: Do you pray very often?

Lisa: Not very often… only when I'm at Zoe's.

Q: Do you pray together?

Zoe and Lisa: Yes.

A lot of Zoe's life outside school revolves around Christian activities. Her family have been to 'New Wine' this year, and are off to 'Greenbelt' in a few days' time. She obviously enjoys the social life offered by the church youth group, and has many friends there. Her own faith seems to be moving from that absorbed by this very Christian upbringing and family atmosphere, and slowly beginning to emerge into a personal faith. Lisa's only contacts with the gospel are through Zoe, and her school. This is a key age, when many young people drift away from the church, and the challenge for the church is how to stay relevant to young people at the same time as sharing the good news about Jesus.

Case Study: Sam

We interviewed Sam at school during his lunch hour. He is also in Year Six, but his family history is very different from the girls' secure ordinary families. We asked him to describe his family.

Sam: There's just me and my dad at home. I've got two stepsisters, but they've gone down to London.

Q: How are they related to you?

Sam: Well, before my dad had me, he met this lady, and they got married and stuff – I don't really know the rest!

Q: Have you met your sisters?

Sam: No, but my dad tells me about them. I'd like to meet them.

Q: What about your mum?

Sam: She died, five years ago.

Sam was happy to talk about his memories of his mum, and how sad he had been when she died, but seems quite content now with being cared for by his dad. He is very aware of his dad's feelings, and mentioned that it had recently been the anniversary of his mum's death. This had made his dad sad, and Sam had tried hard not to argue with his dad at that time.

His family circumstances have an effect on the activities he does.

Q: What happens at the end of the day, after school?

Sam: Well, my dad works, so my friend picks me up and takes me back to her house.

Q: Do you do activities after school, like football or cubs?

Sam: No.

Q: Is that because you don't want to, or because it would be difficult for your dad to pick you up afterwards?

Sam: No, it would be fine.

Q: What about at weekends – what do you like doing?

Sam: Just go out with my dad, have a good time, swimming and stuff… go down to the park, see my friends because they are local. And see parts of the family, see my uncles and stuff.

Despite what seems to adult ears to have been a traumatic childhood, Sam appears to have few worries or problems. We talked about school.

Q: Have you started thinking about SATS in class?

Sam: Yes, we did this practice paper the other day, about spiders. It was OK.

Q: And what about secondary schools – do you know where you want to go?

Sam: Yes, I want to go to T—

Q: Why do you want to go there? Have you been there?

Sam: No, not yet. But I like the school, and some people that I know are there. I've got a niece who goes there.

Q: Do you think it's a good thing that it is a mixed school, that girls go there too?

Sam: Yes, I reckon. Most of the people I know are girls.

Q: Is that because you prefer being friends with girls?

Sam: Yes, because you get someone to talk to. Sometimes you don't get people to talk to you, if they are boys.

Q: Would you say most of your friends are people from school?

Sam: Yes. Some from near where I live.

Q: Are you allowed to go out to the park or other places with your friends?

Sam: No, only if I was with someone else older than me. About 12 or 13, I suppose.

Q: Have you got a girlfriend?

Sam: No.

Q: Would you like to have a girlfriend? Is there someone you would like to go out with, say at the Sixth Year Disco?

Sam: I don't come to the school discos, I don't know why.

Q: Do you think girls worry more about stuff like girlfriends and boyfriends than boys do?

Sam: Maybe.

Sam seems completely uninterested in the things which had fascinated the girls – relationships, fashion and music. His dad chooses his clothes, and he is uninterested in whether he looks fashionable or not.

Q: If you had £10 to spend, where would you go? What would you spend it on?

Sam: I wouldn't spend it, I'd save it for a car or a job when I get older.

Q: Do you ever spend money on yourself?

Sam: Well, my dad buys me anything I need.

Q: Does he give you pocket money?

Sam: Yes, and I save that.

Q: Have you got your own bank account?

Sam: Yes.

Q: What was the last thing that your dad bought you?

Sam: Some books – a selection of J K Rowling books. Harry Potter books, I enjoy them.

Q: Is reading one thing that you enjoy doing at home?

Sam: Yes, I read any books, and comics.

Q: What sort of comics do you read?

Sam: *The Simpsons* and stuff… just comics that I like, that have free stuff on the front.

Q: Do you watch much TV? What is your favourite TV programme?

Sam: *Eastenders*.

Q: Why do you like it?

Sam: It's just about tragedy. It's got good actors in it, I like the actors in it. I like people that are being nice to each other.

Q: Have you got terrestrial TV, or have you got extra channels?

Sam: Yes, I've got cable.

Q: What channels do you watch?

Sam: Cartoon Network, Nickleodeon. My dad watches football.

Q: Do you watch football?

Sam: No, I don't like it.

Sam has had some contact with a local church, through his neighbours. His dad works with one of his neighbours, and one day they invited him to a church service.

Q: Do you like coming to church?

Sam: It was alright. That was the first time. I am a Christian, but I never get to church, I don't know why. But I still read the Bible.

Q: Where did you get your Bible from?

Sam: My dad bought it for me, because he knew I would be a Christian.

Q: Does your dad ever go to church?

Sam: He used to, before he had me though.

Q: So is your dad a Christian? Do you ever talk about it to him?

Sam: Sometimes.

Q: You've been along to the church club on Monday nights too, haven't you?

Sam: Yes, but only once.

Q: Why did you only go once? Was it rubbish?

Sam: No, it wasn't rubbish. But I was round at my neighbours' house because they were helping me out with some maths, giving me extra lessons, and I was feeling upset one day, so they said did I want to come out to the club, and I said yes.

Q: Do you pray?

Sam: Yes, I pray at school sometimes. I prayed when we had that minute's silence, you know when the Twin Towers were attacked. God helps me with things, He's got me over some things, like when we had a maths test I got 19 out of 20 the other day.

For Sam, the ideas he has about Christianity are all positive ones. He has very limited contact with church, but happily calls himself a Christian and tries to read his Bible and pray. He said that the part of the Bible he reads most often is the Ten Commandments, and sometimes he reads about Noah's ark.

Children between the ages of 8 and 10 cannot usually make decisions for themselves about where they go on a Sunday morning. If churchgoing is not part of their family's way of life, it is very unlikely that a child will be able to start attending a group run on a Sunday. For Sam, the main contact he has with Christians is through his neighbours, who are helping him out in practical ways. However, despite a lack of formal teaching about God, Sam's understanding of the Christian faith seems good and he spoke with assurance of his relationship with God. As we seek to reach the children around us, let's expect God to be always surprising us! He may well have got there first!

CHILDREN AND THE CHURCH

Chapter Five – Walk the Talk

In the first section of this book, we thought a great deal about children. We considered their spiritual growth, the ways they learn and the world they live in. So, we know quite a lot about 8–10s in theory! How do we use that knowledge to underpin the work we do with them in churches? How can we put together a programme of activities that draws on our understanding of 8–10s and thus offers them the opportunity to learn more about God's love for them? We need to link our thinking about children with what we actually do. Theory is meaningless unless it informs our practice, and practice is less likely to succeed if it is not underpinned by theory.

Any mission statement your church writes in relation to its work with children is likely to include the desire that they come to own the Christian faith for themselves and that they grow in that faith. Rightly so. But what exactly can we do to help children from whatever background to actually be in a position to accept Jesus for themselves? How do we translate our overall aims into a programme of activities?

There are many different types of groups for 8 to10-year-olds being run by churches. We cannot hope here to offer a definitive programme for them all! Instead, let's look at some principles that will help you to put together a programme for your specific group.

Where are we now?

Imagine two very different children's groups. One is a group of 8 to10-year-olds who meet every Sunday morning. Almost without exception these children come from church families. Their parents worship in church whilst you work with the children in an adjoining hall. The other is a group of 30 8 to10-year-olds who arrive at your church hall every Wednesday evening. They come straight from school and are a mixture of children from church families and the friends they have invited. We have established that we want children of this age to make some decisions about God. We want them to start to think about the things they do in their everyday lives in the light of what they understand about God. But the two groups themselves would require very different starting points along the road to achieving this aim. The activities on offer in each case would be different because the aims of the group would be different. Let's look at how we might identify some specific objectives for a group.

Does your church have a mission statement? Is there a separate mission statement for the youth and children's work?

Look at any mission statements written by your church. They provide the overriding principles for all you are doing with the children you work with.

Now:

Can you write a mission statement that is specific to your group? Use it to summarise for yourself and others the overall aims of the work you are doing.

Our mission statement:

Whether you are working with an existing group, or your church believes there is a need to start a new work, find out what's on God's agenda! In this modern climate of strategies and objectives, it's easy to get caught up in ways of planning that push God out, believing that our man-made systems alone can identify what we need to do. God might have entirely different ideas. Only by seeking his will can you undertake seriously the steps that follow.

Identify a need

This might be a need to begin a group, either for children already attending your church or as an outreach to unchurched children in the community. It might be a need to develop an existing group. You might want your Sunday morning group to understand more about prayer, or to take a more active part in the services they attend.

Look at your resources

- Be realistic. You might have a vision for an after-school club that attracts up to a hundred children a night, but if you only have two or three volunteers this simply isn't going to happen! Think about:
- what time you have available
- the space you have to work in
- the available leaders.

Also think about what other churches in your area are doing. Too often churches work in isolation, trying to do everything themselves. At the same time, the church down the road is launching a similar project and struggling for leaders too. What might happen if the resources were pooled and the vision was shared?

Draw up some objectives

This is where the temptation to be over-ambitious creeps in. You need to hold on to your overall mission statement but you also need some specific objectives for your group and these need to be manageable and achievable.

For example, if you are beginning with a group of unchurched children, your aim of seeing them grow in faith is a long term one. It is work that cannot even get underway until they have the beginnings of a faith to draw on. So what might your objectives be? They might look something like this:

- To provide a safe place for children to be together.
- To develop social skills between children.
- To build strong relationships between children and adults.

These aims, if fulfilled, will lead to the kind of environment where children feel safe and valued. This is an environment that fosters openness and trust. It might well lead to the possibility of introducing Jesus to these children in a low-key format that allows them room to challenge and ask questions. Only after these foundations have been carefully and patiently laid might the aim of seeing children grow in their relationship with God even begin to seem possible.

Look at the action plan below. Notice how the mission statement informs the specific objectives for half a term, and how the key activities are designed to work towards the objectives. The action plan still allows for the group to follow a published teaching scheme, but ensures the focus is clearly on the objective for that half term.

Then use the blank format on page 91 to write an action plan for your group for the next half term. Keep it handy so that you can check that you are planning activities that will help you meet the objectives. At the end of the half term, review your plan to see how things have gone!

Group: Sunday Explorers	Half term: Sep–Oct

Mission statement / overall aims

- To help children explore and respond to God's word in the Bible and grow in their relationship with Jesus.
- To provide a safe environment for children to ask questions to develop their understanding of the Christian faith.

Objectives for this term

- To look at what the Bible has to say about prayer.
- To explore different ways of praying.
- To see how God answers prayer.

Key activities

- Use LIGHT material. Choose Bible activities that get the children really looking at the text to see what it teaches them.
- Introduce one or more different ways of praying each week (responsive prayers, prayer wall, praying in pairs, circle time prayers etc).
- Keep a group prayer diary so we can see together how God answers prayer.

If your aim is to help your Sunday morning group to understand more about prayer, there is still a need for some specific objectives. 'Understand' is a somewhat abstract term. You need to set down some aims that will provide tangible opportunities for the group to learn about and practice prayer. So your objectives might look like this:

- To look at what the Bible has to say about prayer.
- To explore different ways of praying.
- To see how God answers prayer.

Make an action plan

Aims and objectives are great. We can meet together with our co-leaders, and have a good time identifying the needs of our group and writing some fine sounding objectives. Planning how to achieve them is where the real challenge starts! What will we actually do to fulfil these aims?

Children's work is convenient for action planning as it often falls neatly into school terms. This is important because it gives us manageable chunks of time to deal with in our action plan. Aims and objectives need to be reviewed and reset regularly if they are to be effective. This should be a positive thing. As you meet one set of objectives you can move on to a revised set – and know that your group is moving on.

The action plan identifies what you will do to try to meet your objectives. If you want the children to experience different ways of praying, how will you build this into your teaching programme? If you want your mid-week club children to develop their social skills, what kinds of games will you include in your programme to encourage this?

Action planning ensures that what you do week-by-week is working towards the objectives you have set. Don't leave your thinking at the 'aims and objectives' stage, however admirable they might sound. Move on to thinking about how to implement them and your programme will have a defined purpose that is seeking to follow God's will for your group.

This is the point at which you can begin to plan the programme of activities you want to offer the children. We have already seen that the kinds of activities you offer will depend on the group you are leading. Once you are clear about your objectives, it's good to involve children of this age in the planning of a programme. They will almost certainly have ideas for social activities and it's good to run with some of these. If you're working with a Sunday group where your main aim is teaching the Bible, don't be afraid to discuss the format of the session with the children. This age group is the one where giving a level of autonomy and independence to the children can reap rewards.

Group:	Half term:

Mission statement / overall aims

Objectives for this term

Key Activities

Planning a session

Let's think again about the two different types of groups we considered earlier and begin to make some decisions about the content of the sessions that you might plan for each. We've broken the sessions into the stages outlined by Marlene LeFever's model, just so you can see how it works in practice.

Sunday groups

Take the Sunday morning group that you want to learn more about prayer. Let's imagine you have between 45 and 60 minutes for a typical session. You need a specific aim for a session so that you can be sure your activities are actually teaching the children what you want them to learn.

Stage 1: So, if your introductory session on prayer is intended to teach the children that prayer is about communicating with God, you need to spend the first ten minutes or so introducing the theme – how do they communicate with each other, what do they think prayer is? Remember, the first five minutes are crucial in establishing what the session is about, so the activities you choose are important. A game or craft activity might be appropriate, followed by a discussion when the children brainstorm their understandings of prayer.

Stage 2: The biggest chunk of time will need to be given over to looking at what the Bible has to say about the theme. Limit the amount of material you look at in one session so that the children get a clear understanding of perhaps one specific passage, rather than a series of disjointed references studied out of context. Use the material below about teaching the Bible to generate some ideas. You might spend some 30 minutes on this part of the session, but remember that this shouldn't all be one activity if you want to maintain the children's attention. You might look at the passage and see what questions the children have about it, keeping these in mind as you study it together. This might be followed by a retelling of the passage in another form – as a drama, a choral reading… whatever is most appropriate for the particular passage under discussion. A quiz might follow to check understanding of key details. Different passages will require different combinations of activities; what matters is that this crucial part of the session holds the children's interest and gives them the opportunity to explore the passage together.

Stage 3: If you've spent time looking at what the Bible has to say about prayer, you will want to spend some time doing it! Leave up to 15 minutes at the end for this. How you do it will depend on the passage you've been looking at. You will need to decide if it is right to use an approach that is noisy and full of praise, or more reflective and thoughtful! Again, there are many suggestions to help you decide.

Chapter Link

In Chapter Seven we look at the 'mechanics' of running a group. Look here for more information on resources and recruiting volunteers.

Playing games can be a useful ice-breaker, and they are lots of fun. But they can be more than that – they can be a way of introducing or reinforcing a theme and create experiences that help people to learn, grasp concepts and take ideas on board. Try some of these books to get you started:

Lesley Pinchbeck, *Theme Games 1*, SU 1993 and *Theme Games 2*, SU 2003 Two books of games designed to introduce children to biblical themes.

Patrick Goodland, *Over 300 Games for All Occasions*, SU 1998 Packed full of games for outdoors and in, parties and parachutes – and every other kind of game you can think of!

Ruth Wills, *Everyone's a Winner!*, SU 2001 200+ cooperative games and activities for use with 7–13s

If you're looking for more inspiration for activities of all kinds for your midweek club, take a look at: Jan Dyer, *100 Children's Club Activities*, Kingsway Website: www.kingsway.co.uk

Over a period of weeks with a group like this, you will want to keep a balance of activities. However exciting the group finds doing drama, it will become tedious if you do it every week and they come to expect it. Similarly, they need to know that there are different ways to pray, and that within the safety of a group they will enjoy the opportunity to explore these together. So it's always good to plan an overview of a series of sessions rather than just one at a time, so you can keep an eye on the balance of types of activity.

Midweek groups

Your midweek group will require a different balance of activities altogether, because your objectives for the group are different. Whilst we hope that, of course, your Sunday morning group will have fun too, this is a key emphasis with the midweek group, because you want them to develop relationships with each other and the leaders that help to foster an environment where sharing Jesus with them becomes a natural step forward.

So an hour-long session with this group might still have a theme to it, but the balance of activities might be different. Imagine your theme is about 'rules'.

Stage 1: With your Sunday group, you might do a simple activity that highlights the importance of rules as an introduction to a series on the Ten Commandments. With your midweek group you may well spend the first 30 minutes or so of an hour-long session playing games. They will be games where knowing the rules and playing by them is important – and the focus will be on having fun together, because that's a key objective for this group.

Stage 2: But maybe then you will have a 15 minute slot when the children sit down with a drink and a biscuit. You talk briefly about why the rules of the games were important and share a little about the rules God has laid down for us that are also for our benefit and because he loves us and wants the best for us.

Stage 3: The evening might finish with a final ten minute activity – perhaps a simple craft with clear instructions to follow, to reinforce the good results that come from following rules or instructions.

The emphasis of activities in these two sessions is very different. The key is that in each case the make-up of the session is determined by the kind of group it is and the specific objectives for that group. Each session takes account of the needs of the children, and it is their needs that determine the depth of Bible teaching.

If you are involved in a midweek group, look back at the aims and objectives you identified for this term. Are there any changes you could make to the way you currently run the session that might help to achieve these aims more effectively? Make some notes below – and then read on into the next chapter where you will find some more ideas!

So whilst we can't design a 'one size fits all' programme for you to use with your group, we can look at the key elements of a programme for 8–10s and think about how to do them with this age group. Your action planning and knowledge of the children will inform the balance of activities and the approach with your particular group, but let's look at some principles and some practical examples in a number of key areas.

Using the Bible

Whatever kind of group you are involved with, you will want to use the Bible with them. This might be on a weekly basis with your Sunday morning group. It might be at an introductory level with the children in your mid-week club. But the Bible is central to all that we do. We can't leave it out no matter what form our work with children takes. So, how do we do it?

The Bible is a book essentially written for adults and we are seeking to share its truths with the children we teach. Taking this responsibility seriously means thinking through an approach that will do this effectively. It means taking our own personal Bible study seriously – after all, if we don't have a sense that God's Word is vital and relevant for us today, we'll have trouble communicating that to our children in our group. Knowing that we take it seriously, watching us as we use our Bibles, will speak volumes to them before we say a word. It also means taking time over the preparation of a session with your 8–10s.

We are often nervous of tackling the Bible with children. Some of it troubles us as adults, some of it seems too difficult for them to take on board at such a young age, and we want to avoid facing questions we may not be able to answer. While these concerns are valid, we can use the Bible with children.

Rosemary Cox suggests that we need to keep two important tasks in mind as we teach children the Bible. Firstly, we need to help them to understand the 'big story' that can be seen from an overview of the Bible – the story of God's community. We need to help them to begin to see their part in the ongoing story of God's people. Secondly, we need to help them get to grips with the 'variety of types of teaching material, set in different literary forms, with differing teaching goals' (Rosemary Cox, *Using the Bible with Children*, Grove Books, 2000). A challenging task – but is it achievable?

There are all kinds of ways to explore a Bible passage with your group and we've listed some of them below. Reflect on the passages you will be teaching to your group over the next month. Which approaches might be most useful? Resolve to try out some new ideas!

As a radio or TV interview – have a leader play the role of a reporter describing an event from the Bible. Interview children in role as witnesses.

Turn an account from the Bible into a radio play, adding appropriate sound effects.

Use drama – get the children to mime an account as you read it, or to make tableaux of key parts of the story. Prepare a script for the children to read in parts or get them to improvise.

Give the children key elements to listen out for before the story starts, eg 'Who said…?' 'Why?' 'What happened after…?' etc. Use their responses to help recap the story afterwards.

Or give them particular words to listen out for – they join in with a response or do an action when they hear the words.

Use puppets – the children can make them and use them to tell the story – maybe they can even perform it to younger children.

Tell the story as a monologue – use a leader in the role of a Bible character.

Tell an 'active story' where different parts of the room are set up as different parts of the story. This is great for stories that involve more than one location. Use simple props to mark the different areas. Simply tell the story or act it out together.

Read aloud or follow the story in the Bible – then have a quiz to reinforce key points. Or get the children to design their own quiz, making up questions for each other, or for adults who have been learning the same passage!

Use different versions of the Bible: children's versions, *The Message*, the Contemporary English Version.

Try telling the story as a rap, or a poem.

Use a video of the story (see Scripture Union's resource catalogue for a range of videos).

Use musical instruments – compose a piece to tell the story.

Use a parachute – great for stories that involve stormy seas!

We thought a great deal about how children learn in Part One. Keep that in mind as we now consider teaching them about the Bible. This book tells an incredible story of God's plan for his world, uses a diversity of literary forms – historical narrative, poetry, parables, literal and pictorial language – to achieve its task, and seeks to teach us God's truth in a variety of ways. For all these reasons the Bible is in one sense ideal for sharing with 8–10s! We have already established that children learn in different ways and we have agreed that we want to offer them diversity in the ways that we teach them. The genres of the Bible allow us to do this and we need to share it in such a way that our 8–10s see for themselves a role in God's plan for his world. We must draw on their natural inquisitiveness, their sense of adventure and their creativity – all that God has made them – in order to do this.

We need to encourage them to engage actively with the material we present to them. In every other area of their development, as they try to make sense of the world around them, we seek to give them helpful experiences, teach them to ask the right kinds of questions, support them in their attempts to make sense of something new. We can do this with the Bible too.

Naturally, we may worry that the nature of the Bible is too complex for them to grasp in all its diversity. Different kinds of literature require different approaches and adults find this difficult too. For example, what should we take literally and what is figurative or abstract? Yet the very nature of teaching – particularly in Literacy – in our schools right now encourages children to grapple with texts in a way that was once reserved for secondary school education. Children are only too aware that not all types of text are the same, and that the way we read them must be different.

Because of this, it's fine to let children explore the text and begin to make their own discoveries. If they can actively engage with the material we present to them, they can begin to make sense of it for themselves. We do not always simply want to 'deliver' biblical truths to them and expect them to accept them unquestioningly. Try to set up activities that encourage exploration and questioning attitudes. Use some of the questions in the Action box opposite as a starting point for this. Ask these kinds of questions with the children as you explore the text together, so that they can begin to ask similar questions of the text themselves to develop their understanding.

We need to create an environment where it is safe to ask questions, to disagree, to explore ways of living out the truths they discover. Children of this age are just beginning to question and explore. They begin to have an understanding of concepts that are more abstract and outside their own personal experience.

Helping children to ask questions of the Bible material we are trying to teach them means allowing them to ask and answer the kinds of questions Rosemary Cox suggests in *Using the Bible with Children* (Grove Books, 2000):

Narratives:
'Was this a story which someone (for example Jesus) told, or does it record a real event?'
'When and where were the events happening?'
'What else was happening elsewhere in the world at that time?'
'What were people's everyday lives like then?'
'Are there any words I don't understand?' (eg centurion, Samaritan)

Poetry:
'What was the writer feeling?'
'What did they want to express'
'What are some of the key images being used?'
'Why?'
'How would I express the same feelings?'

Letters:
'Who sent it?' 'Why?'
'Who received it?'
'What are the main issues?'

For the most part they remain satisfied with the answers of those they see as positive role models and authority figures – but we must work hard to be real with them and maintain their trust. Encouraging their questions and being honest when the answers are not clear cut is important in helping them to develop the ability to question and reflect as they move on in their understanding. We must use all that we have discovered about how children learn to help us develop methods of teaching that engage their interest and help them to make sense of the material they encounter. Then we will be laying the foundations they will need as they continue in their Christian faith.

Of course, it's important to note that whilst we will do all we can to facilitate an open atmosphere that will enable children to engage with the Bible text for themselves, sometimes it will be appropriate for us to step in and correct a clear misunderstanding of the meaning and context of a passage. Clearly, we cannot interpret the Bible to mean 'anything I want it to mean' and we'll want our children to grow up with a clear understanding of the truths at the heart of our faith.

Some important principles

The learning cycle that we explored in Chapter Three is a helpful approach to use when trying to unpack the Bible. Children need to see a relationship between what we want them to learn and the world they live in. They need to see how it applies to their life. So, start by building bridges between the world of the children and the Bible material you want to share with them. Remember the importance of the learning context and find ways of engaging the children's interest as you introduce the theme.

Remember that the worlds of the Old and New Testament are dramatically different to the world of your average 8 to 10-year-old! They will need opportunities to get to grips with the historical context. Ask them what they don't understand, be prepared to go away and find out more about the customs and traditions of the time, and make available some of the excellent books written for children on the subject.

What follows is by no means an exhaustive list of resources! There are literally hundreds out there and you need to be clear about your particular needs before you buy. But these should get you started!

Teaching the Bible:
Look at these published teaching programmes:

X-stream is SU's brand new curriculum programme for 8-11's. It contains loads of helpful ideas and fun activities to get your group praying, worshipping, engaging with the Bible and living out faith in the world today.
Website: www.scriptureunion.org.uk

Trowel, published by the Good Book Company
Website: www.thegoodbook.co.uk

The Children's Ministry Teaching Programme
Website: www.childrensministry.co.uk

Using art and craft:
Kathryn Copsey (compiler), *Here's One I Made Earlier,* SU, 1995.
Christine Orme (compiler), *Here's Another One I Made Earlier,* SU, 2000.
Both these books contain craft ideas for children up to the age of 11.

Praying with your group:
Judith Merrell, *101 Ideas for Creative Prayer* and *New Ideas for Creative Prayer,* SU, 1995 and 2001.
A collection of ideas for helping children to pray. Prayers that can be shouted, sung, drawn, made and joined in with.

Ideas for worship:
Nick Harding has written a training feature on worship with 8–10s on the website www.scriptureunion.org.uk/newsalt
See also his book, *Children can worship* (Kevin Mayhew).

Kidsource (Kevin Mayhew) is a resource book for children.

The Big Book of Spring Harvest Kids Praise (ICC) and other similar publications by Spring Harvest are good sources of new children's songs, and are accompanied by tape or CD.

Brian and Kevin Draper, *Refreshing Worship,* BRF. An alternative look at worship, offering unconventional ideas but asking searching questions about this generation and how what we do in church relates to them

With the context firmly established, introduce and explore the Bible material for the session. Use a variety of different methods for sharing the Bible with children – and engage a variety of senses as you do it. This is the material we want them to really engage with and learn from, so we need to draw on all that we understand about how they learn to make sure we get our message across. Drama, storytelling, quizzes and craft all have the potential to engage different kinds of learners in different ways, so try to have a balance of these activities over a period of time.

Using drama

Drama can take a number of different forms; all of them require the children's active involvement, but to different degrees. It can be rehearsed and polished or spontaneous and improvised role play, depending on the context of its use. If you want to use what the children have done to show others, perhaps as part of the main church service, there will be a different emphasis than if you are using it to explore the thoughts and feelings of characters in a particular Bible account.

Storytelling

Storytelling needs careful preparation but can be a powerful tool. Essentially it involves a leader retelling the Bible passage, but since we have established the need to engage different kinds of learners we need to use techniques that actively engage our visual and kinaesthetic learners too! The use of props, particular words to listen out for accompanied by a required response or action, and actual movement around the room during the retelling are all ways of engaging the children in the material they are hearing.

Art and craft

Picture the scene: your group arrives to find the room prepared with trays of paint and big paintbrushes surrounding a huge sheet of paper made from joining strips of lining paper together with parcel tape. You read them the day's passage from the Bible and they get to work painting a backdrop to be used in church when they perform their prepared drama script to the rest of the congregation. This scenario might fill you with dread if you are the kind of person that doesn't like lots of mess, but the children will love the opportunity to work on this kind of big scale. And more importantly, as they work, conversations about the Bible passage will arise naturally as they make decisions about what needs to be painted onto the backdrop.

And what about those children who love to doodle whilst you are reading them the Bible? Make it legitimate! Let them draw the facial expressions of the characters as you read, or get them to draw the scene as you describe it.

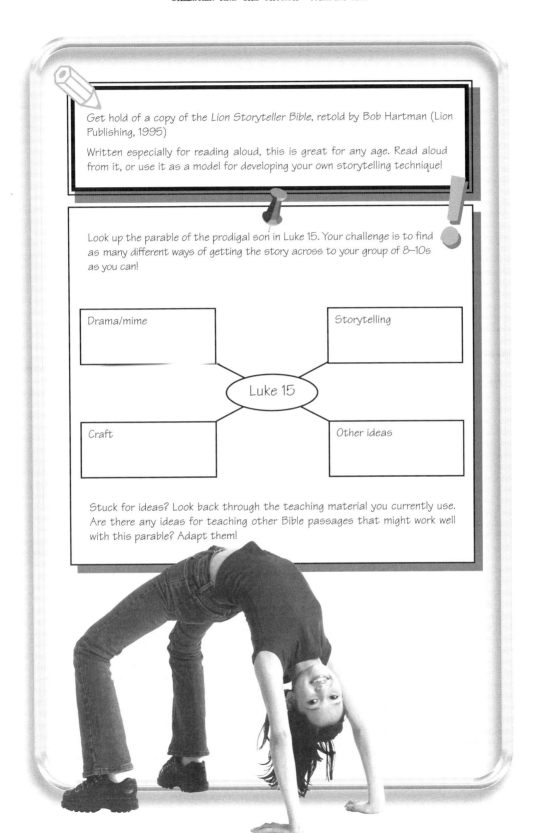

Get hold of a copy of the *Lion Storyteller Bible*, retold by Bob Hartman (Lion Publishing, 1995)

Written especially for reading aloud, this is great for any age. Read aloud from it, or use it as a model for developing your own storytelling technique!

Look up the parable of the prodigal son in Luke 15. Your challenge is to find as many different ways of getting the story across to your group of 8–10s as you can!

Drama/mime

Storytelling

Luke 15

Craft

Other ideas

Stuck for ideas? Look back through the teaching material you currently use. Are there any ideas for teaching other Bible passages that might work well with this parable? Adapt them!

Art and craft activities are a great way to capture the interest of those children who like to be active. Careful preparation is the key. However straightforward to make something looks, make sure you've tried it out in advance. You need to know all the potential pitfalls and you need to know how much time it will take. There's nothing more frustrating for children than a craft activity that doesn't work properly, or something that takes too long to finish.

Don't forget the third stage of the learning cycle. The children need to see clearly how the Bible passage they have studied applies to them and to their life. A large part of this is encouraging them to respond to what they have heard and act upon it. Prayer and worship will play a vital role in this part of the session.

Prayer

Prayer is essential to our relationship with God and we will want our 8–10s to grasp this. Sometimes it's easy to assume that the children we work with know the basics of prayer and the reasons for doing it. Yet as adults we can find it hard to explain these things and it's worth taking time to explain it to children.

We pray because the Bible tells us to (see Philippians 4:6 and James 5:13,14 for just two of numerous examples). We pray because talking and listening to God is a vital part of growing in relationship with him. God wants us to talk to him and he wants to use our prayers to his glory. And so we don't simply want to pray for our 8–10s, we want to pray with them. We want them to see for themselves that prayer can make a difference and we want them to feel able to offer their own praise and thanks to God in ways that are helpful to them.

We need to offer a variety of opportunities to pray in different ways. They need prayers they can shout out loud, they need the time and space to pray quietly by themselves and out loud in a group. They can write, draw, make and sing their prayers. And they must know that all of these are equally valid and pleasing to God. Somehow we need to avoid the message that the long and eloquent prayers that form part of liturgy or that they hear other adults say out loud are better than those that they themselves offer to God.

Practical ideas for prayer

As with the Bible, the context for prayer can be important in making it both memorable and meaningful. If you have just shared the story of Nehemiah and the writing on the wall, asking children to write their prayers and add them to a prayer wall might make a powerful connection for them. Writing prayers of praise and thanksgiving onto leaf shapes and attaching them to a tree will reinforce the message of Palm Sunday. The simple addition of quiet reflective music can help children to be quiet before God and offer him their own silent prayers.

Using the Circle Time format that children are used to in school can be a helpful way to pray for themselves and each other. The very nature of Circle Time is intimate and encourages children to share honestly. Developing a similar approach in your group can encourage the children to pray openly for one another and to share their individual prayer needs. A key feature of Circle Time is the passing of an object around the circle – only the person holding the object can speak, and any child who doesn't want to participate can simply pass the object on. This means that individual children have control over their level of participation.

Helping children to know what to pray for is important too. This is particularly important if we want to broaden their perspective and help them to pray for the wider world. They are at an age when they can begin to relate to things that are outside their own immediate experiences, but we need to help them do this. Recording a news programme aimed at their age group can provide a starting point for discussing national and international situations and praying for them. Using child-friendly literature about mission agencies your church has links with can also be a helpful starting point.

Children are pragmatic – they will want to know that prayer can work! As adults we may well understand the power of prayer and have numerous examples of answers to prayer that we or others have experienced. It's worth sharing these with the children, but it's also important to help them to recognise how and when their prayers are answered. Keeping a group prayer diary can be a good way of doing this. Recording key situations that you have prayed for together and reflecting back to see how God has answered these prayers can give children clear and positive messages about the value of prayer.

Worship

You are the LORD's people. Obey him and celebrate! He deserves your praise (Psalm 33:1).

When you meet together, sing psalms, hymns, and spiritual songs, as you praise the Lord with all your heart (Ephesians 5:19).

Why do Christians worship? Firstly, because God deserves it, and secondly because when we worship together it encourages us and builds up God's people. Why should 8–10s worship? For exactly the same reasons! Many of the children we work with will know Jesus for themselves and be following him every day, and worship needs to be part of their walk with him. Some of them may only just be getting to know God – but the things they are discovering about him should be leading them to praise him – his love, his care and protection for them, his plan for their lives. We may well have children who come to our groups with no personal relationship with Jesus - for them, the worship of others may be just the witness they need. Suddenly, rather than just learning *about* God, which after all they may well do in RE lessons at school, they see people actually engaging *with* God! What sort of God is this, that inspires a 9-year-old to sing, 'My God, you are so cool!'

Worshipping all together

Worship can take place in all sort of ways – hopefully your group will regularly meet with the whole church family, and be part of the body of Christ offering up praise and thanksgiving together. Some churches have thought carefully about all-age worship, and your group will love these times. Other 8–10s may find this shared time difficult, and we need to prepare them for taking part by explaining parts of the liturgy that are difficult to understand, practising a hymn together if it is unfamiliar or learning actions for a song that they can show to younger children. Do any of the children of this age have a voice in preparing for shared times of worship in your church? Is there a way to make them feel more included – perhaps they could write to the person who chooses the music with their favourite songs, offer to lead prayers or prepare some drama for the service. We need to be teaching them too about the needs of the whole church, and helping them see what worship means for everyone. Do you have a musician who would be willing to let your group have a tutorial on the organ or the drums one day, explaining how they work and letting them have a go? Can some of your group shadow the team who run the sound desk, learning how to control the mixer? Who prepares the bread and the wine for Communion, and what happens to it after the service?

Spend some time reading the Bible passages below and reflect on the examples of how worship flows from a teaching session:

Bible base: Job 38

Theme: The glory of God's creation

Worship: Children collect pictures from travel brochures to create a 'Wonders of the World' holiday, or download images into a power point presentation, to create a tour of the places God might take Job to. While they are compiling their picture or presentation, play them a well-known hymn praising God for his creation – for example, 'All creatures of our God and king' or 'Great is your faithfulness, O God my Father'.

Bible base: John 12:1–7

Theme: Responding to Jesus

Worship: In your teaching session, do some role play of this scene and imagine how it felt to be Mary. What was the cost to her of her actions, both financial and emotional? Challenge the group to think about how far they are prepared to go in their response to Jesus, and how much they are constrained by what they feel others might think. Remind them that the group area is a safe place, and experiment with different postures for a simple song like 'Father, we adore you'. Talk with the group about how they feel kneeling, arms raised, swaying etc., and then sing or play the song again as a time of worship, with them choosing movements.

As leaders, we can set the mood by taking seriously times of worship with our group. They are still eager to pick up from us cues about what is OK, so if we feel free to lift hands in praise, to close our eyes, to sit, kneel or stand unself-consciously, we are showing them that it's OK to worship God with our bodies as well as our words.

Worshipping on our own

Many leaders find organising times of worship when the group is on its own embarrassing, awkward and artificial. Maybe we all have in our minds' eye a vision of the Big Top at Spring Harvest, or hundreds of young people singing at Soul Survivor, and feel we can never match that. So we approach worship in a diffident and apologetic way with our group, and needless to say it fails miserably.

Let's look back at the reasons to worship – the first was that God deserves it. Rather than looking at 'Worship' as an extra element that has to be added on to your programme, look instead at God and what you are learning about him. What have you been hoping to share with your group in any particular session? And what sort of response can you all make to what you have learned? That response, in whatever form, is your worship.

Worship can be singing, but if you are not confident in your own singing abilities then it might be better to start with something else. Why not get a few CDs, listen to some Christian music, choose some tracks your group especially like and work out ways to personalise them by adding accompaniments or movements. Or read some of the Psalms, especially ones with an obvious structure like Psalm 148 or Psalm 136, and copy the structure, adding your own words. You can use movement, stillness, smells, lighting, experiences such as a walk by the sea or an early start to hear the dawn chorus as opportunities for worship. There are many books and web-sites which are full of ideas for worship which involve no guitar playing or music reading skills.

Jesus said to the woman at the well:

> 'God is Spirit, and those who worship God must be led by the Spirit to worship him according to the truth' (John 4:24).

All you need to begin to worship with your group is God's Spirit, and the truth of who God is.

Resources

Resources can mean all kinds of things, but let's concentrate on the kinds of resources you might need to help you plan a typical session. The kind of material you need will vary depending on the kind of group you are leading. A Sunday morning group aimed at nurture and discipleship will quite obviously require different resources to a midweek club that focuses on a variety of games and activities with a short teaching slot at some point. Establishing clear aims for the group you are leading will help to determine the kinds of resources you need to get your hands on.

Spend some time in your local Christian bookshop, talking to worship leaders at your church or browsing online to pick up some good resources for worship. A few places to start are:

www.kingsway.co.uk

Kingsway are a major music publisher, and will even let you listen to samples of music online. Titles to look out for include

- *Children's Praise and Worship*
- *12 New Children's Praise songs*
- *The Nation's favourite Hymns*
- *Songs of Fellowship for Kids*

www.springharvest.org

Each year Spring Harvest publishes CDs from its conferences, such as:

- *Kids Praise 2003*

www.vineyardmusic.com

This is a good source of contemporary Christian music. Try:

- *Great Big God*
- *Fruit of the Spirit*
- *Change My Heart Oh God for Kids*

- Have a 'Listening Spot' as a regular part of your Sunday session or midweek club time. Ask children, leaders, mums and dads or other adults in the church to bring in a track from a Christian CD to listen to together. Encourage them to talk about why they like it, when they play it, whether it helps them to worship God etc.

- Organise a CD library, so that children can borrow CDs to take home. This is an idea the whole church might want to take part in. You could launch it by asking everyone to buy a copy of their favourite CD to donate to the library.

There are essentially two possible ways forward in terms of teaching resources:

1 A published teaching programme

A ready-made teaching programme from a Christian publisher means you are buying into the expertise of the people who produce it, which should mean a carefully co-ordinated programme underpinned by sound educational theory. This gives you the peace of mind to simply concentrate on the delivery. There are a couple of health warnings, however. Using a published teaching programme does not cut down on preparation time – you need to know the material inside out to teach it well. Also, a published programme won't be specifically tailored to your particular group. You may need to adapt it to their needs.

2 DIY resources – planning your own curriculum

Some churches prefer to plan and prepare their own material. It's best if this is a decision that is wider than just the 8–10s age group. A whole church approach means that a broad and balanced curriculum can be designed that is not repetitive and builds on what the children know as they work through the age groups. The result: a programme tailored to your group that fits in with the core values of your church.

However, such an approach requires a team of people committed to the task: a mix of people with creativity and imagination as well as those who are comfortable with identifying aims and objectives and lesson planning. So it helps if at least some of the people involved have an educational background.

This is also a long-term project that will take time to develop and it is a time-consuming approach for people who are often already heavily committed in other areas of work and church life.

An approach that lies somewhere between the two may well be the answer. A pre-published resource gives you a clear structure and a selection of activities to choose from. But don't be enslaved by it. Use other resources with supplementary ideas and activities. Books of games, craft ideas, responsive prayers are all out there and mean that you can tailor any programme to the needs and preferences of your particular group.

Using Bible reading notes

Children in the 8–10 age group are usually independent readers so now is a great time to encourage them in their own personal Bible reading. Some children will be from Christian homes where this is the norm, but others will not.

Making it something you talk about in the group can really help. Look together at the range of notes on offer for this age group and maybe even get the church to buy a particular set of notes for the group. Then you can commit together to reading the notes during the week and including some discussion of them in your weekly session.

If you are choosing a published teaching programme to use, get some samples first, and make a thorough comparison before deciding which to invest in.

Ask questions such as:

- How prescriptive is it? Do I get to make choices based on my knowledge of my particular group?

- Is there a range of activities suggested so I can make sure I plan a programme to address different learning styles?

- Is there material to deepen my understanding of the Bible passage before I teach it to the children?

- Does it allow children to ask questions and make their own interpretations of the biblical text?

- Does it give a sense of the 'big story'? Over a period of time will the children get a sense of God's plan for the world?

- Does the material help children to make links between the Bible material and their own lives?

- How easy is it to follow? Are instructions for activities clear and straightforward?

You can probably think of other things you would want to know, based on your situation and experience. Don't make a rushed decision!

Beyond the group...

We have focused in this chapter on how we might plan our work with our group, but we need to think briefly about how we see our work with children in the context of the wider church. Children need to make sense of the world around them and they are quick to pick up on hypocrisy and injustice! No amount of teaching in a small group of children their own age will have any significant long-lasting impact if the same children's experience of their place in the wider church community is not one of feeling that they belong and are loved. The whole church needs to see that it has an important role in teaching children. We need to work together with the leaders and members of our churches to ensure that our work with children is continuous – in services, in social events and in their groups they must see, hear and experience same message about God's love for and acceptance of them.

Are there opportunities in your programme for sharing with the rest of the church community – all-age services, a Passover meal, a dramatic retelling of the Christmas or Easter story? These are just examples of the kinds of activities that lend themselves easily to be shared together as a church family. What is important is that the wider church community has opportunities to learn together about our place in God's plan. Children who experience active involvement in their age-group work will not appreciate being talked at whenever they meet together with the rest of their church family. Remember how they learn best and allow them active participation on these occasions too.

All these things give the children the message that they have a place in the church family now, not just in the future. It means that what they learn about how God values them will make sense to them in the context of the wider church.

And finally...

This has been a chapter of ideas. We hope it has inspired you to try some things with your group that you may not have tried before. We hope too that it has helped you to develop a clear longer-term plan for the work you are doing with them. You know your group best and it is our hope that this chapter will have helped you in the task of tailoring the programme you plan for them to the unique needs of the particular group of children God has entrusted you to work with.

How involved is your group in the wider life of the church? List some ways that they're involved?

What ideas has this chapter provoked about ways to increase and broaden their involvement? List some of your ideas and plan what you will do about them.

Is there someone connected to your church who works in another culture or nation? When they last visited your church, what did you do to involve the children in learning about their work? Was there an opportunity for them to talk to the children too? Children of this age are fascinated by the wider world with its diverse and colourful cultures.

We can use all that we know about how they learn to prepare for a visit from someone working there. Prepare a display, find out about the music, dress, education of the country concerned and help the children to think about what they would like to find out from their visitor, so that they can ask questions if they have the opportunity. Keep the display for use during future weeks, updating it when possible and encouraging the children to pray for the work.

Chapter Six – Sunday Morning… and Beyond

In Bournemouth, on every Saturday morning of the football season, a junior football league comprising somewhere in excess of 150 teams gets underway. It was set up by a local URC minister who wanted to run the league on a Saturday morning to ensure children were free to attend church on a Sunday, when most other such football leagues regularly take place.

This was a move of a man with vision. His desire was to see children in the churches of Bournemouth on a Sunday morning, and he took positive action to try to make that vision possible. Traditionally speaking, church is on Sunday. So it is a natural assumption that this will be a key time for working with children in our churches too.

But is this a fair assumption to make anymore? Let's spend some time looking at and reflecting upon what really is happening in our churches in terms of working with 8–10s. We're going to consider four case studies and then explore some of the key issues they raise for us all.

Case study 1 – an urban church

Take a large church in an urban setting. It has a Youth and Children's Pastor and, numerically speaking, a thriving work amongst young people.

During the week there are two key meeting times for the 8–10s. On a Sunday morning the children meet in the hall that adjoins the main church building. They have a time of teaching whilst the adults are in church, joining them for the latter part of the service, which has an 'all-age' feel to it. Many of the same children, some of their school friends and a high proportion of children from the small housing estate opposite the church centre, meet on a Friday night for an evening of fun activities.

The two meetings have distinct aims. Attendance at the Sunday morning group is mainly children whose parents are church members. The overall aim is simply to teach the Christian faith. The leaders seek to offer a supportive learning environment that encourages the children in their own faith, wherever they are at, and which enables them to ask and explore their questions. The group mainly follows Scripture Union's teaching programme, which uses a mix of learning activities to teach the Bible. Within this overall framework the leaders are able to set objectives for their particular group in the way we described in Chapter Five. This is an element of planning that the Youth and Children's Pastor is trying to develop within the work.

Make some notes as you read through each case study in this chapter. What is good about each example? Can you see any weaknesses? What kinds of children might be reached through each particular way of working? Are there any issues or concerns that the case studies raise in your mind? Jot down anything at all; you will refer to it again as you read on through the chapter.

Notes:

On Fridays the overall aim is to build up relationships between the children and with the leaders. The focus of the evening is on having fun together and a typical evening includes a ten minute warm-up game, followed by the main activity (a typical term's programme might include a games night, an arts and crafts evening, a quiz night, cookery or a swimming trip). After the main activity, tuck and drinks are served and the evening ends with a 'thrash about' – a last fast and furious ten minute game to use up any remaining energy! The club takes place in the church centre at the heart of the local community. As a result the club draws in unchurched children from the surrounding area as well as the children from the church. The group has no specific spiritual input, except at Christmas and Easter, though the leadership team is considering whether to introduce this on a more regular basis, as it is something that has worked well within the club setting of the 11–14s group.

Both groups share the same name, and each publicises the activities of the other. There are a number of church children who attend both sessions, but the leadership teams are different. Occasionally an unchurched child from the Friday night group may also attend a Sunday morning meeting. The Friday night group is seen as an evangelistic opportunity, although the Youth and Children's Pastor is aware that specific objectives need to be set if this opportunity is to be used effectively.

During each summer holiday the church aims to run a holiday club. The children in both groups are encouraged to attend and to bring a friend. The aim is to show that Christians can have fun together. It is also part of a strategy to build relationships between the Friday and Sunday groups, and to build up both groups.

Case study 2 – a rural church

One church in a rural area had seen its Sunday group decline until there were just four children from church families who attended on a regular basis. The church wanted to broaden its contact with other children in the area and looked for advice about how they might do this. One piece of advice they received, in January 2000, seemed rather unorthodox – to close the Sunday group! But this was exactly the course of action the church took. In April of the same year, once a month on a Sunday the church began to run a club to which they invited children in the area.

There are all kinds of examples of exciting and innovative work that is going on with children in our churches. We have picked just four typical examples here. Two useful books that explore some more radical models of working with people of all ages in churches today are:

Michael Moynagh, *Changing World, Changing Church*, Monarch, 2001

Stuart Murray and Anne Wilkinson-Hayes, *Hope from the Margins – New Ways of Being Church*, Grove Books, 2000

Notes

_____

_____

_____

_____

_____

_____

_____

_____

_____

_____

_____

_____

_____

_____

_____

_____

Using holiday club teaching material they developed the club-style approach and began to see up to thirty children once a month. This led also to increased contact with the parents of these children. The following July, just over a year after the club began, the church ran a one day mission event to which they invited all the children who had contact with the club, and their families. Sixty children and their families attended the mission, and the parents heard a presentation of the gospel. The church sees little of the children and their families other than in relation to the club. But many of the parents hang around during and after the club, so contacts are being made with local families.

Case study 3 – a midweek club

The results of a survey undertaken by members of a Christian Centre in a small village showed a lack of activities for young people in the village. Concern about this, and the desire to do some effective outreach amongst these young people, led to the opening of a midweek club for 8–10s. This group's success meant that a similar project with 11–14s is now thriving alongside the initial group.

One of the aims of the club is to build relationships with and amongst the children by providing a safe environment where they can feel loved and accepted. But this midweek club has another aim too: to present the gospel to the children, leading to commitment, growth and discipleship.

This second aim affects the programme of activities on offer each evening. It retains a number of elements of a midweek 'social' club, such as that in Case Study 1. For example, there is a tuck shop and the programme includes a range of games and other activities. But there is also a theme for the evening that aims to teach the children about Jesus. The session is presented in a series of ten minute slots, some of which involve using the Bible and praying. The leaders are each allocated one or more ten minute slots to prepare, and other leaders are then available to work with small groups, so that effective relationships can be built up. This is the pattern of the club for two out of every three weeks. The third week is an activity with no overt spiritual input.

A few children in the group also attend the church Sunday group, but most do not. The club and the Sunday group are not directly linked. As the children from the 8–10s group progressed into the older group, several made a Christian commitment. A Bible study for these young people began at the home of one of the leaders. One of these young people is now integrated into the adult fellowship. Of those who are now too old to attend the 11–14 group, half have joined the church's youth cell group.

Notes
_____
_____
_____
_____
_____
_____
_____
_____
_____
_____
_____
_____
_____
_____

Case study 4 – a multi-cultural area

In an area with a large Asian population, an SU worker has made contact with the local school. She is involved with the Christian assembly there (the school runs different assemblies for children of different faiths) and also provides support for some lessons. Once a week she runs a girls' club, attended by Sikh, Hindu and Muslim children, as well as other children of no faith. She has two Hindu helpers. The girls play games, do crafts, chat and listen to music. There is a low-key Christian element each week: the children hear a Bible story or learn a memory verse. They do not pray together and no assumption is made that the children have any knowledge or experience of God. Here the aim is about relationship building – through the club deeper relationships have been developed with these girls than would have been possible purely through assemblies and lessons. Because of this, the children have begun to talk and ask questions about the Christian faith.

Time to reflect

The examples we have considered above are very different. Each of them responds to the community in which it exists, offering something that works, at least to some degree, for them. We expect, too, that each case study will have raised some questions or issues in your mind and we hope you have jotted these down. They may be things that excite or concern you about each of the projects we explore. Or there may be elements of one or more of the projects that have challenged you to think in new ways about the work you are doing in your own church. As we explore some of those issues together now, look back at what you have written and ask God to help you see what he might be saying about the work in your church.

It is important to be clear at this point that no one model of working with this age group is right or wrong. There is no 'one size fits all' approach that we can offer as a solution to all your problems. Every case study we have considered has important strengths, just as each one raises some interesting questions. We need to reflect on these issues, and then consider our own situation, with the aims and objectives we identified in the last chapter, as we seek to discover how we might best work with our 8–10s in our own individual situations.

Write a case study of the work with 8–10s in your church. Try to identify your aims, and describe what happens during your meeting times. At this point, just stick to the facts and avoid making judgements about the work.

But first, if you attended church as a child, think back for a moment to your own experiences. Naturally these will be different for all of us. You may come from a Christian family that attended church together every Sunday morning. You may instead remember being dropped off at Sunday School by parents who then went home and returned to collect you later. You may recall formal, teacher-led lessons where Bible knowledge was imparted for you to learn and remember, or you may have experienced the beginnings of the more informal, active approaches we have explored in this book. Church may have been central part of your life throughout the week, or it may have been just a place you attended on Sundays.

Whatever your memories, it is likely that your experiences of church as a child were shaped by the community within which your church existed and the wider culture of society at the time. We have spent a great deal of time considering the world in which children live, the kind of education they receive and the kinds of pressures they experience. In the light of all that we have discovered, we cannot simply assume that the ways we have always worked in our churches remain relevant for today's children. The case studies have already hinted that some churches are beginning to think differently about how they work with this age group. We must look at how we respond to the changes in our communities and our wider culture as we seek to reach these children with the gospel.

Asking new questions

Let's begin with our first case study. In many ways, this is a traditional way of working and it has some important strengths. Many churches have realised the value of a midweek club that runs alongside the Sunday morning work as a means of offering church children a safe place to bring their friends and have fun together. We have seen that 8–10s are at the point of beginning to ask challenging questions, and of looking for role models outside their immediate home environment. This traditional model clearly aims to create an environment where children are safe to ask questions of adults they trust and who provide positive role models for them. In our case study church the consistent attendance at both the Friday and Sunday sessions is a clear signal that the model is working well for them.

But the crunch comes when we ask how many of the unchurched members of the Friday night club make the transition to attending the Sunday group as well? The answer is very few. So we may ask ourselves:
How we can make these children come on a Sunday so that we can tell them about Jesus?

If you want to go beyond the case studies and broaden your thinking about the possibilities of working with children in your community even further, then check out the 'KidzKlub' model, based in the work pioneered at Metro Ministries in New York.

Under the 'KidzKlub' model work with children has two key parts – a weekly meeting involving Bible teaching, worship and prayer, and a weekly visit to each child's home to build relationships.

Visit www.trinity-church.org.uk and click on kidzklub to find out more.

But this question contains some important assumptions. The majority of us who attended church as children were taught about Jesus on a Sunday morning. It's always been that way. It may be that we expect to work with children in the same way as people worked with us. If so, we have perhaps inadvertently assumed that we need to tell children about Jesus on a Sunday. It's time to consider what's really important – that we tell them about Jesus on a Sunday, or that we tell them about Jesus, full stop.

It's time to ask a different yet very simple question with some huge implications:
How can we tell children about Jesus?

Within that one question we have begun a shift in thinking that no longer asks how we fit these children into our existing structures, but instead asks another important question:

What kinds of structures might effectively meet these children where they are?

And so we have begun to ask new questions. What we need now is some new answers. But why? What is it that causes us to ask these questions at all?

Facing Facts

A drop in numbers in your existing group of 8–10s or a realisation that what you are doing is not reaching the unchurched children in your area may be a catalyst for asking questions about the work you're involved in. This kind of thinking was what caused the churches in the case studies we described above to make changes in existing approaches or start something new and different. Whatever the catalyst, such realisations mark the point at which the new questions we identified above cannot be ignored.

It seems somewhat glib to simply say that times have changed but it's true. In his challenging book, *Changing World, Changing Church*, Michael Moynagh argues that it's time for the church to face facts. He states unequivocally a truth that may well have been niggling away at many of us for some time, but that we have struggled to voice:

> Many clergy and lay people know that today's church is not working, it is not connecting with people anymore, but they cannot imagine anything different. They struggle on with tried and trusted methods, feeling uneasy but with little vision for how things could change.

Let's face some facts about the children we want to share the gospel with that might shed some light on why 'tried and trusted' methods may be less effective than they were.

We asked some of the children we worked with in schools two questions about prayer:

- Do you ever pray?
- Do you think God answers prayer?

Here are some of the answers they gave:

- [Prayer] is silly. God's not real.
- There's no such thing as God so you're talking to nobody.
- I don't think God always answers prayers.
- If they say there's such a thing as God then who created him?

Our Sunday morning work with children often works from the premise that the children who come have some church background. The children who gave the kinds of answers above were from church schools, but their families did not attend church.

Would your Sunday morning group effectively meet the needs of children who either believe that God is not real, or have a limited knowledge of him?

As you read on, prayerfully consider how you might meet the needs of such children in your community.

The nature of Sundays

How did you spend Sundays as a child? Again, there will be a number of different answers but you may well recall it as a day when your parents didn't work, perhaps as a day when you sat down together to a roast dinner and when you did other things together as a family. In some senses at least you probably remember a day that was more restful (or perhaps more restrictive!) than other days of the week.

But the traditional nature of Sunday as a rest day has gradually been eroded. Earlier chapters in this book have explored the nature of the world in which our 8–10s grow up, and many of the issues we have highlighted are implicit in the reasons Michael Moynagh cites for the decline of the traditional Sunday congregation. We all know that less people are in church on a Sunday morning. We may well lament that fact, but we need to look at what they are doing instead. The high separation rate amongst parents means that weekends are a key time for visiting absent parents. The fragmentation of the family means that weekend visits to grandparents and other relatives are an important part of family life. And for those who are not away from home, the nature of Sunday has become one of sports and leisure pursuits once confined to weekdays and Saturdays. Bournemouth's Saturday football league is not the norm; Sunday has become the traditional time for many similar such leagues. Whether we like it or not, churches today compete in the market place with all kinds of alternative Sunday activities.

If we hold on to our traditional belief that Sunday is the only time for teaching the Bible to our 8–10s we will simply not reach those children who have never heard about Jesus before. In Case Study 1, the Youth and Children's Pastor has begun to look at how the midweek club might provide a more effective means of outreach. The leadership team is in the process of introducing a ten minute 'Time-out' slot to the club night, which will provide weekly spiritual input to all the children. Answering difficult questions does not always mean making radical changes; the answer may be a much simpler adjustment to what is already happening.

The church that runs a midweek club in Case Study 3 has achieved a balance between its two aims of building relationships and teaching the Christian faith. As a result children from completely unchurched backgrounds feel comfortable attending and they receive clear Christian teaching within a relaxed environment. And once every three weeks they receive no overt spiritual input at all. But the leaders would want to argue that there can be times when the children learn as much about Jesus during these weeks as on any other. And since we have seen that children look at adult role models and expect what they see to match up with what they have been told, the episode described opposite would suggest that they are right!

The episode described below happened during a midweek club session where no overt spiritual input had been planned. It is described by one of the leaders:

'We had been teaching the group about choices they make and having to take the consequences. We wanted them to see that they could not blame anyone else for their choices – we often hear 'but they made me do it' from young people, and we were trying to get them to take responsibility for their actions.

'At the last event of the year, a BBQ, we were at a friend's house. There is a stream/river that runs through their garden. The young people and leaders were playing hide and seek, around the trees, bushes etc. After playing about ten games without getting Mark [one of the other leaders], I challenged them to have one last game and the purpose was to get Mark out.

'They worked hard and just as Mark was getting to the tree that was home, about six of them saw him and chased after him. Mark came to a fence and was cornered, so he jumped the fence not realising that the river was the other side of it. He slipped and went in the river. He was covered in wet, mud and algae!

'The young people looked horrified and came and stood by me. "We're really in trouble now," they said. "Look what we made Mark do."

'I was able to point out to them that it was Mark's decision to jump the fence – they did not make him. He had to take the consequences for his actions. Mark could not blame them for something that he had chosen to do. Mark came over the fence laughing and they realised they were not going to get told off! They learnt more in that situation than in any organised teaching slot and enjoyed seeing Mark being hosed down!!'

Reflect on the learning that took place here. It could never have been planned!

Something like this won't happen every time you plan a social activity. But ask God to help you see and use these opportunities when they arise!

The midweek club is here to stay because the nature of Sunday has changed beyond recognition. Thirty years ago we took our children to Sunday School. Today we take them to swimming, football, ballet… the list is endless. Taking a child to a midweek club run by the church fits this pattern of life much better than a Sunday group. If we want to reach these children we may have to teach them the Bible midweek.

The nature of church

Let's think again about the midweek club we described in Case Study 3. The church that supports the club has seen minimal success in integrating the children into the wider life of the church. Very few of the children from the club also attend on a Sunday morning. Despite their attendance in midweek, the church itself remains something of an alien culture.

Or consider the girls who attend the club described in Case Study 4. They are making early explorations of the Christian faith together. But if one of the Sikh, Hindu or Muslim children wanted to attend church on a Sunday morning, that simply may not be an option.

The rural community in Case Study 2 has seen thirty children regularly attend its monthly club morning. Their family mission day attracted large numbers. However, these children are not seen at church at any other time and their parents continue to make contact through the club without being brought into the main body of the church.

Yet all three case studies document examples of effective contexts for telling children about Jesus. All three have provided a different answer to the question of how to tell children about Jesus. What they have in common is that they have answered the question by starting with the community in which they are based and responding to its needs. Perhaps too often we expect the people in our community to come to us and fit into our existing structures rather than considering what might happen if instead we went to them, started from where they were and met their needs. The result might be far from traditional, but it may be more effective than anything we have tried before.

Case Study 4 is an example of a group run in a school in a multi-cultural area. Working in these areas raises its own unique issues. Scripture Union has a multi-faith adviser who can be contacted at the National Office:

Scripture Union
207–209 Queensway
Bletchley
Milton Keynes
MK2 2EB

Telephone: 01908 856000
Website: www.scriptureunion.org.uk

Working in schools is a ministry that is important to many churches in building links with the community.

Running Christian Groups in Schools: Practical Help and Resources for Working with 5-12s by Esther Bailey is published by Scripture Union and looks at issues concerning working with schools, as well as containing over 40 ready-to-use outlines.

But would it be church? Is church just what we do on a Sunday morning? Are we only happy to support the kinds of work we have described in our case studies provided the ultimate aim is to help the children 'progress' to Sunday morning attendance? In short, if the nature of Sunday has changed, is the nature of church changing too?

The gospel hasn't changed, and we must not pander to today's postmodern society by allowing God's truth to be manipulated, distorted and compromised in the name of 'acceptability'. But if our ways of being church are not radical and effective, then the gospel is not reaching out to those who need to hear it. Tough questions need to be asked and answered through the exploration of new and innovative ways of working. Whether we like it or not, and however frightening it may seem, our culture is changing. It will not stop changing simply because we ignore it. So how do we move forward?

Back to the Bible

For your church, one of the case studies above may already be engaged in the kind of work you know is the next step for you. You may already have identified a need as you drew up your action plan in the last chapter or in your jottings during this chapter. Or it may be that the whole concept of moving away from traditional models is something your church has never considered. There is a radical shift in thinking that needs to take place before such a concept could work for you.

But before you do anything else, consider what the Bible has to say. We need to be sure what the non-negotiables are before we plan new projects. If we fail to do this we lay ourselves open to the danger of following society at the expense of the truth of the gospel. Before you go any further, work through the material from Acts 2:42–47 and Acts 4:32–35, using the questions opposite.

In 1 Corinthians 2 Paul tells the church at Corinth that when he was with them he 'resolved to know nothing … except Jesus Christ and him crucified' (verse 2, NIV). If we resolve to teach our children 'nothing … except Christ and him crucified', we need to be careful that we are not tempted to add to this teaching by attaching conditions to the gospel.

For example, if you work with 8–10s in a midweek setting, think for a moment about how the rest of the church views this work. If we consider the key themes of the passages in Acts that we studied earlier, we may consider that what happens during a midweek club such as that described in Case Study 3 can be seen as a valid expression of 'church', but this may not be how it is viewed by others.

Read Acts 2:42–47 and Acts 4:32–35 – a picture of the early church. What were its characteristics?

- Learning together (2:42).
- Meeting together – fellowship (2:46). Notice that such fellowship took place in both the formal setting of the temple courts and informally in each other's homes.
- A community (2:45; 4:32–35).

Based on these principles, could your children's group be regarded as a form of church?

It may be that sometimes we seek to add to the gospel by accepting these children as part of the church only if they attend on a Sunday morning and participate in a service that is our expression of being 'church'. As a result, it may be only a matter of time before we are simply hanging on to our traditional expressions of church, whilst our children disappear from our numbers.

But if we view church as the gathering together of God's people for the purpose of spurring one another on in relationship with him and modelling him to the world, then developing the Christian element of the clubs in case studies 1 and 4 could become 'church' for these children. In all of these settings we could see elements such as worship, prayer, teaching and fellowship being worked out. The same could be said of the club in Case Study 3, where the children spend one evening a week learning together from the Bible. In some sense at least all these examples might be described as 'church' – but not as we knew it!

This is new thinking that raises tough new questions about the nature of church – and such questions will not be answered overnight. We are not suggesting that you make instant radical changes to your work with 8–10s. Instead we simply urge you, as you address your action plan, to consider the issues and ask God to show you what they mean for your work in your church.

Start talking

Talk to God first! But talk to others too. Some in your church may share your concerns, others may never have considered the issues we have explored but be willing to listen. Use outside agencies such as Scripture Union to brainstorm ideas with and to find out what other churches are doing. No project undertaken by one church can simply be replicated in another area. But there will be shared underlying principles and it is good to see how another church has tackled a similar issue.

As you talk, go back to your action plan, and identify specific, manageable changes you might make. If you need to start a new work, go back again to Chapter Five, work through a new action plan and be clear about what you are trying to achieve before you start. None of the projects we considered in our case studies came into being overnight. Each responded to a need in a specific community by praying, discussing and planning together before the work began in earnest. Also, any work like this needs to be owned and supported practically and in prayer by the whole church body and the leadership.

Go back to your case study of your own work with 8–10s. What are its strengths? Whose needs does it meet? Are there issues about the nature of Sundays and the nature of church that are relevant to your work? What changes might be needed to make your work more effective? How might you begin to address these issues?

HEALTH WARNING!

You cannot change the world overnight! Prepare a plan that moves you forward in manageable and realistic steps.

This is an important principle. It can be easy to read about what other churches are doing and assume they are big churches with lots of financial and human resources. But the churches we've described in our case studies by no means all fall into that category. They have started with their own unique situation and asked God to show them how to respond to the needs of their community. What they share is a willingness to move beyond existing traditional structures as they seek to reach the 8–10s living in their area with the good news of Jesus Christ.

A challenge!

This has been a chapter of questions! That is because we write at an exciting and challenging time for the church in our culture, a time when there are many more questions than answers. But it will take the courage of some churches in some areas to explore these issues through the projects God calls them to undertake, before we see where God is taking his church in the future.

We urge you, wherever you stand in your thinking right now, to seek God's will for the children in your community – and pray for the vision to meet that challenge.

Chapter Link

Consider again the passages from Mark's gospel we referred to in Chapter One:

Mark 10:13–16
— We must ensure that we do not let anything get in the way of children meeting Jesus.

Mark 9:42
— God does not look favourably on those who obstruct or hinder a child's relationship with him.

Reflect again on those two passages and use them to pray about your work with 8–10s.

- Give thanks to God for the good things you have identified about the work you are doing.

- Praise God for the children in your group who have a relationship with him.

- Ask God to show you if there is anything about your work that may be hindering children from meeting with Jesus.

- Ask him to show you the changes you can make to prevent this happening in the future.

- Ask for the courage to be radical if that's what's necessary to move forward.

Chapter 7 – Nuts and Bolts

One of the things that children of this age group love to do is the quizzes in magazines that are supposed to reveal what type of person you are. You know the sort of thing:

Are you a good friend?

Q 1 Your friend comes to school with a disastrous new hair-do. Do you:
a) lie and tell her it looks great?
b) suggest she comes round to your house after school and you do each other's hair?
c) tell her you hate the way she looks – you've promised to always be truthful to each other?

Well, maybe how you read this chapter tells us something about you. Did you:
a) turn to it first?
b) leave it till last?

If you answered (a), maybe you pride yourself on being a practical person. You have not got time to read a lot of theory; you are more interested in getting things done. Perhaps you can see the needs of your group only too clearly, and are hoping for some help to solve them. Perhaps you have got into difficulties in the past, and want to know more about child protection, health and safety or training new leaders.

Please go ahead and read the chapter, and we hope it answers some of your questions or suggests places to look for advice. But then go back and read some of the others. Because prevention is better than cure, and maybe by spending some time thinking about the young people that you work with and the God who has put you there, you can avoid some of the problems ever happening.

If you answered (b), that could just be because this section is near the end of the book! But it might be because you are the sort of person who loves reading, thinking and talking about a project, but baulks at actually doing something. Every team needs someone to be the ideas person, the inspiration, the one with the spark – but it also needs those who will get things done. And one of the reasons for writing this chapter is to make doing things less daunting. Let's learn from each other, and from those who have been this way before. You may hope that you never need to know some of the things included here – but at least take time to skim through them so that you know where they are if you are ever faced with dealing with them.

The kingdom of God needs thinkers and doers: and so do God's children.
Let's look at some mechanics!

Find someone who is a childminder, works in a playgroup or nursery, or has taken children on a school trip.

- Talk to them about the paperwork and regulations involved and how they felt about it.

- Has anything ever gone wrong for them? How did they feel then? Have they changed any of their procedures since?

Talk to a parent who leaves their child with a childminder, at a playgroup or a nursery. How do they feel about the rules and procedures?

- Do things change as children get older?

- What does it mean to be in loco parentis?

Matthew 14:14–21

When Jesus got out of the boat, he saw the large crowd. He felt sorry for them and healed everyone who was sick.

That evening the disciples came to Jesus and said, 'This place is like a desert, and it is already late. Let the crowds leave, so they can go to the villages and buy some food.'

Jesus replied 'They don't have to leave. Why don't you give them something to eat?'

But they said, 'We have only five small loaves of bread and two fish.' Jesus asked his disciples to bring the food to him, and he told the crowd to sit down on the grass. Jesus took the five loaves and the two fish. He looked up towards heaven and blessed the food. Then he broke the bread and handed it to his disciples, and they gave it to the people.

After everyone had eaten all they wanted, Jesus' disciples picked up twelve large baskets of leftovers.

There were about five thousand men who ate, not counting the women and children.

What does this passage tell us about Jesus' concerns for people?

Are they practical or spiritual?

Recruiting leaders

Many churches have a problem recruiting enough people to lead their children's groups. What do we mean by enough? What is the ideal number?

For children of 8 to 10, there should be a ratio of 1 adult to every 8 children. In an ideal world, I wonder what your criteria for those leaders would be. Perhaps you'd be looking for at least one leader of each sex. It would be good to have at least one trained first-aider. There should be someone musical to lead worship, someone who can explain the Bible, someone who is sporty and can organise games, someone with counselling training, someone from an ethnic minority… well, we can dream!

In the last analysis, however, we are doing God's work so, along with the legal and practical requirements we inevitably have for our children's leaders, let's see what other criteria God has.

Character and commitment

Titus 1:7–9 talks about those who have responsibility in the church. Your children's workers are in a position of great responsibility so there are some principles here that will apply to them.

> *Since an overseer is entrusted with God's work, he must be blameless – not overbearing, not quick-tempered, not given to drunkenness, not violent, not pursuing dishonest gain. Rather he must be hospitable, one who loves what is good, who is self-controlled, upright, holy and disciplined. He must hold firmly to the trustworthy message as it has been taught, so that he can encourage others by sound doctrine and refute those who oppose it. (NIV)*

Notice that this list says nothing specifically about the person's skills. It does have a lot to say about their character. We should beware of taking the view of the world when we consider a person, simply looking at what skills and talents they have which seem to make them right for the job. Samuel made this mistake when he went to the home of Jesse to anoint one of his sons as the next king of Israel. God had this to say to him:

> *Do not consider his appearance or his height, for I have rejected him. The LORD does not look at the things man looks at. Man looks at the outward appearance, but the LORD looks at the heart (1 Samuel 16:7).*

Work as a group.

Look at this list, and add any other words you can think of. Then prioritise the words — try to put them into three columns: 'essential', 'desirable' and 'unimportant'.

A children's leader should be:
Patient
Artistic
Reliable
Honest
Guitar-playing
Computer literate
Committed
Forgiving
Fit
Female
Single
Under 30
Churchgoing

Clever
A football fan
Fond of children
Funny, having a sense of humour
Able to use a photocopier
Male
Self-controlled
Humble
Experienced
Able to sing
Christian
In good health
Married
Clued-up on youth trends

Obviously, skills and training are incredibly valuable. We would actively encourage you to look at how you can equip and train children's leaders in their work, increasing their knowledge and practical skills. But it's equally important that our children's leaders are people of godly character. Don't overlook people who may not immediately seem to have all the skills you require. Lots of these can be learned.

Looking out for workers

Church should be a place where people are not just brought into the kingdom, but discipled when they get there. The issue of finding leaders to work with children is just one part of the way the church can encourage Christians to find out how God wants them to serve him. All of us are in the process of growing and learning. Many American churches continue to have 'Sunday School' for adults – and in the UK, the idea of adult education or learning for life is becoming more and more popular. Is this hunger for learning and desire to develop evident in our spiritual lives too? When was the last time we read a Christian book (apart from this one!) Have we made any progress in our prayer life over the last year? Are we asking God where he wants us to serve him now?

If a church family is healthy, there are elders, home group leaders, discipleship groups or pastoral carers who are encouraging each person to find their own spiritual gifts – and to find ways to use their gifts to serve one another. If work with children is seen to be an integral part of your church's life, where children are regularly involved in worship, prayed for and shared with, and the adults are being challenged to grow in their faith and look for ways of serving God, the area of children's ministry will be recognised and actively plugged as a great one to get serving in! Until then, we need to get down on our knees and pray for Christ-like eyes, to see the people around us as God sees them and see their potential. And we also need to put into place a programme to train and support leaders and anyone who shows an interest.

Matthew 9:36,37

> When Jesus saw the crowds, he had compassion on them, because they were harassed and helpless, like sheep without a shepherd. Then he said to the disciples, 'The harvest is plentiful but the workers are few. Ask the Lord of the harvest, therefore, to send out workers into his harvest field.' (NIV)

What was Jesus' advice on how to tackle a shortage of leaders?

Look up these verses:

Exodus 4:10–13

Judges 6:14–221

Samuel 3:1–10

Jeremiah 1:4–10

Were these people confident about doing what God was asking them?

Sometimes when we approach people to ask them to take on some leadership role, their response may well be negative. We need to learn to trust God and be patient with his timing. Keep praying for those you have asked, and encourage them if you genuinely can see they have the skills you need. Suggest they come and observe the group, or they visit for a specific purpose such as sharing their testimony or helping with an outing. But don't put too much pressure on them and be prepared for them to say no.

Employing a children's worker

Many churches reach a point where they consider employing a full or part-time worker to develop their youth and children's work. If your church is at that point, read on to help you begin the process of making an appointment.

Do we need a children's worker?

It is perfectly possible to reach a point where the children's work in your church needs to be led, co-ordinated and developed further and there is a need for someone with the vision and the gifts to take on this role. Then your reasons for making an appointment may look like this:

'We need someone to give a clear vision for our work with children.'
RESULT: Everyone in the church knows what we are aiming to do amongst the children in our church, leading to prayerful support for the work.

'We need someone to co-ordinate and develop our volunteers.'
RESULT: Volunteers are recruited and feel supported and equipped in their work.

'We need someone to identify ways of expanding our work amongst children.'
RESULT: Clearly identified priorities are established and the work can be developed according to the needs and resources of the church.

However, it's crucial to think this through. There are at least a couple of reasons for employing someone that are at best unhelpful, and yet they may well account for some churches' decision to make an appointment:

'We need someone to do the work for us.'
This might really mean, 'We have real trouble recruiting volunteers, and we'd quite like to free up some of those we do have to do something more important instead.'
PROBLEM: The worker begins with a set of unrealistic expectations and an unmanageable workload.

'A church like ours should have a children's worker.'
This might really mean, 'Other churches of our size have someone, so it would look good if we did too.'
PROBLEM: The expectations for the worker are likely to be unclear, quickly leading to frustration on both sides.

Be careful that the reasons your church comes up with aren't actually cleverly disguised versions of the above!

How do we go about it?

Be professional. Draw on the expertise of church members, denominational advisers and interdenominational organisations who have experience of making appointments. These people know how to draw up job descriptions, shortlist applicants, interview, appoint and induct new members of staff. It's a complicated process that's not for the inexperienced, and there is a wealth of expertise available.

Have these churches thought about what they want?

Is it clear from the adverts if they expect someone to work with children (under 12) or youth (12+)?

From the responsibilities laid out in the advert, could you imagine what a typical week's work might be for the successful applicant?

Are the expectations of these churches reasonable?

St Clueless, Anytown, Anywhere
Is looking to employ a Children's Pastor to coordinate our youthwork.
This person will:
- Recruit, train and support volunteers in our Sunday School.
- Coordinate outreach and mission amongst the youth of the area.
- Lead assemblies, RE lessons and Christian Unions in our local primary and secondary schools.

St Clued-Up, Sometown, Somewhere
We are looking for a committed Christian who is passionate about children's work and has relevant qualifications and/or experience:
- To work with 3–11s, heading up a strong team of volunteers.
- To equip, encourage and support members of the congregation to be involved in children's work.
- To begin to explore links with local schools, identifying opportunities for outreach.

Put together a realistic package. Devise a clear job description and person specification so that everyone knows what you are looking for. Think carefully about the kind of salary and accommodation package you can offer. The obvious vocational nature of the work is not an excuse for a meagre salary. Look at comparable jobs in the secular world, and investigate the kinds of packages being offered by other churches. Consider the qualifications and experience you are looking for and seek to offer the kind of salary that will make it possible for such applicants to make ends meet! Make sure you make proper provision for time off and annual leave. Ensure you have a clear process for ongoing training and pastoral support.

Manage the worker you appoint. The process doesn't end when the appointment is made. Think about how you will achieve a balance between supporting your worker and making them accountable. The structures you need will depend on the previous experience of your worker – but make sure the structures are there. Without them frustrations and misunderstandings that hinder the work will inevitably set in.

We want professional and gifted people to work with the young people in our churches; there is no excuse for us to be anything other than professional in our employment procedures.

With a worker in place for the right reasons and with clear objectives and priorities, you might expect to see:
- a valued and supported worker.
- a valued and supported volunteer force.
- clearly planned provision for your young people.
- young people growing in their faith and reaching out to their friends.
- an expansion of the ministry into new areas.
- more young people coming to know Christ.

When the priorities are right, God's work can be done – unhindered.

Training and support

Why is training important?

It has long been recognised in the world of business that a company's most valuable assets are its personnel. Companies seek to attract top quality staff by offering flexible working hours, good rates of pay and all manner of perks. Things are very different, however, in the voluntary sector. The church is not alone in finding it increasingly difficult to recruit volunteers. Our local Brownie pack faces closure this autumn when Brown Owl retires – and they have not been able to find anyone willing to take her place. There seems to have been a big change in attitudes from Brown Owl and her generation, all close to retirement, and today's 20s and 30s who might have been expected to take over running, among other things, the Sunday children's groups. Words like 'duty', 'service' and 'commitment' are no longer important to us. Instead, we are fed the messages 'What's in it for me?', 'What will I get out of it?', and 'I don't need any more stress'.

Amaze

PO Box 5898

Hinckley

LE10 2YX

www.amaze.org.uk

This association of Christian youth and children's workers produces a manual to help you in the appointment of a worker:

The Amaze Employment Manual

The Christian message of course runs counter to this, but we cannot ignore the fact that many of our potential or existing youth workers are products of their culture. Rather than grumbling that people should be helping out with young people's groups, then wondering why so few appear to want to, or leave disgruntled after six months, we need to ensure that we are taking their needs into consideration. Perhaps we can learn a lesson from business – after all, we believe in the value of each person not because of the profit they might earn us, but because of the huge price that God has already paid for them. But if we truly value them, our treatment of them needs to show this. We need to listen to what they need, and be perceptive enough to hear those needs that they don't always voice. Those needs are likely to include both specific training, for example in discipline with 8–10s or in first aid, and more generally feeling valued for what they do, having a rota which gives them some time off and having an evaluation and review procedure which ensures they can air their feelings.

The way in which you train and support your team will vary according to how many people are involved, what previous experiences and skills they have and who you have available to do the training!

Where do we start?

Let people know about the training when they first start. Ensure they know how important it is. If you have a monthly team planning meeting for example, make sure they know when it is and that they make it a priority. Don't try and pretend to them that the level of commitment is going to be lower than it really is.

Have a rota which enables each person to have some 'time off', and if possible have a floating volunteer who can cover so people feel they can have unplanned absences too without letting you down. We can sometimes be nervous about using rotas because we have concerns about continuity, and it's true that a badly managed rota can be damaging. But for children of this age it can work. They are becoming more adaptable, can handle working with different adults, and may even look forward to it. It may well be starting to become part of their school life to be taught by more than one teacher, as some schools set for different subjects and many primary schools use jobshares. If you need to use a rota the key is communication between the leaders. Careful planning and consistent expectations mean that such an arrangement can work well.

Imagine…

Following an announcement in the church notice sheet for new volunteers to help with the 8–10s group on a Sunday morning, three people approach the vicar. As you eavesdrop on their conversations, would you have any concerns about these people? What training, support and accountability would you put in place before taking them on?

Mrs A has been heard loudly expressing her views on modern parenting. She tells the vicar she would have no problem keeping the children under control, given the chance.

Mr B is a single man in his 20s. He has no close friends in the church, and the vicar is unaware of any previous experience he has working with children.

Miss C has come to faith through a recent Alpha course. She has worked in playgroups and after school clubs locally. She enjoys aromatherapy and yoga.

Chapter Link

Chapter Six reviews some models of working with 8–10s and asks you to think about your own work. Look at the case studies in the light of the workload for leaders. How would you build in space for time off? How would you ensure leaders are being spiritually fed? Are there opportunities for them to be part of the adult congregation?

Think about their all-round need for support. You might put on specific events to equip them for working with children, but who is supporting them in their prayer life, in reading the Bible, in being married/single/lonely/in debt, etc? Is there a home group, an older couple or a prayer group that could take them on?

Involve all sorts of people in your training programme. Your children's leader may do most of it, but think about involving your minister, your worship leaders, other churches locally, organisations like Scripture Union, or others in the community like the local social services, sports coaches or head teachers.

Make sure the rest of the church knows what is going on. Involve the young people with their leaders in services. Have photos of the leaders alongside those of overseas missionaries, etc. Encourage members of the congregation to ask leaders how it is going, invite them round for a meal, thank them and pray for them. Make sure your leaders are not asked to take on other responsibilities as well.

Ensure there are clear lines of communication, and that leaders feel that their voice is heard. Encourage your minister to come sometimes to planning or review meetings. Make sure everyone knows who they can turn to for advice, ideas or even grumbles! Make sure too that everyone is clear about budgets and spending.

Child Protection

We have already seen something of the world that children live in, and identified some of the dangers they encounter. The issue of protecting our children is one we need to take seriously in our churches, and the difficult area of child abuse cannot be ignored.

What are the key issues?
1) Protecting children:
How would a child seek help in your church if they were being abused?
What procedures does your church have for supervising activities and appointing workers to reduce the possibility of abuse occurring within the church?
2) Protecting children's workers
How can you minimise the risk of false allegations being made against paid or volunteer workers?
How do you counsel, care for and if necessary discipline those whose behaviour is sometimes inappropriate?

The issues are complex, but your church must have a policy for dealing with them. It's a bit of a minefield to say the least, but thankfully there is a wealth of material available to support you in getting it right. Do not even begin on such a policy without drawing on this expertise.

The issue of Child Protection is complex and it's best to look to your particular denomination for specific advice, or to use one of the umbrella organisations listed below.

Churches Child Protection Advisory Service
PO Box 133
Swanley
Kent
BR8 7UQ
0845 120 4550
Email: info@ccpas.co.uk
Website: www.ccpas.co.uk

CCPAS produces an invaluable resource, *Protecting and Appointing Children's Workers* which will help you put together a clear and comprehensive policy. They will also comment on your draft policy and work with you to make it effective.

The Churches Agency for Safeguarding also offers advice and resources to support your Child Protection Policy.

Website: www.churchsafe.org.uk

Amaze has helpful advice on the subject of Child Protection.
Website: www.amaze.org.uk

In the Church of England, most dioceses have guidelines to follow. Contact the diocesan children's adviser for your diocese. The Baptist Union of Great Britain publishes its own book, *Safe to Grow.*

Website: www.baptist.org.uk

The United Reformed Church provides a wealth of information on its website, at www.urc.org.uk

The Methodist Church has published *Worth Doing Well* (Methodist Publishing House).

Chapter Link

Look back to Chapter One to see how much God loves children – part of our responsibility must be to keep them safe from harm.

What needs to be in a policy?

Different agencies will differ slightly in the advice they give, but there are some key headings to consider when drawing up a policy:

Definitions

There are four defined categories of abuse – Physical Injury, Sexual Abuse, Neglect and Emotional Abuse (Department of Health, *'Working Together under the Children Act 1989'*). Make sure these are clearly defined by your policy.

Responding to allegations of abuse

Hard as it is, this must include procedures for dealing with allegations of abuse made against church leaders or members.

Supervision of activities

The level of supervision must be such that the risk of abuse occurring is minimised.

Appointing workers

You will need a policy for recruiting both paid and volunteer staff that ensures appropriate checks are made.

Why should we be concerned about Child Protection?

As Christians and as a Church we are called to recognise the unique position of children. We must respect them as individuals, in their own right and take all steps possible to protect them. Jesus is very clear about the consequences for those who abuse children. In a nutshell, children matter to God. Children are important to God, for who they are. We will be held accountable for how we treat them.

'Unpleasant as it may be, we have to accept and acknowledge that child abuse, in all its forms, does happen. It does happen to Christians. In some cases it is perpetrated by those working for the church, or who are members of the church.'
'Child Protection' – Winchester Diocese Guidelines and Procedures

Health and Safety

The children rush back into church to greet their parents when their group finishes. Mrs Smith greets her twins with alarm. One is bent double, struggling to catch her breath.
'Daisy, calm down. Where's your inhaler?'
Daisy can't answer, but her brother chips in helpfully, 'Her spare one has run out, but they didn't know 'til they looked in the cupboard.'
As Mrs Smith finds another inhaler in her handbag and sits Daisy down, she catches sight of Tom's hands. They are covered in red blisters.
'Tom, what happened to you?'
'Well, we had to go into the kitchen to find some more squash, only I don't think the bottle I found was squash…'
Mrs Smith's face is grim as she marches the children out of the church, stuffing the leaflet they brought with them into the bin on her way out. The words on the top say 'JESUS LOVES YOU'…

The Health and Safety Executive have a helpful website: www.hse.gov.uk

Think about the children, and the buildings you meet in. With your team, run through a typical programme and imagine some 'worst-case scenarios' (see ideas below).
What would you do?
Would everyone know what to do?
What needs to change?
Make an action plan, setting deadlines and responsibilities.

- A leader faints.
- You are tasting food, and a child with a nut allergy goes into shock.
- A child goes missing.
- There is a fire.
- A child has an epileptic fit watching a video.
- Someone different comes to pick the child up, and the child is unwilling to go with them.

Jesus says:

'Don't be cruel to any of these little ones! I promise you that their angels are always with my Father in heaven.' (Matthew 18:10,11).

We chuckle shamefaced at a scenario like this – because for many of us, it could all too easily happen in our church. What we say to the children who come to us will mean nothing if we are not caring for them properly – and that means taking seriously issues of health and safety. Daisy and Tom's problems could so easily have been avoided – which makes them all the more tragic.

Where do we start?

It is vital that someone takes responsibility for health and safety. It may be helpful if it is not someone who is part of your team, because they can look more objectively at the buildings and the procedures you use, and spot any hazards. The Health and Safety Executive has these helpful definitions:

Hazard means anything that can cause harm (eg chemicals, electricity, traffic etc).

Risk is the chance, high or low, that someone will be harmed by the hazard.

They advise carrying out a risk assessment, in five steps:

Step 1: Look for the hazards.
Step 2: Decide who might be harmed and how.
Step 3: Evaluate the risks and decide whether the existing precautions are adequate or whether more should be done.
Step 4: Record your findings.
Step 5: Review your assessment and revise it if necessary.

You should be aiming to make all risks small. If you discover a potential hazard, you need to ask 'Can I get rid of the hazard?' In our example above, one solution would be to ensure chemicals in the kitchen were always in a locked cupboard. If you cannot get rid of the hazard, for example with Daisy's asthma, ask yourself 'How can I control the risks so that harm is unlikely?' This might involve someone checking the first aid supplies regularly.

The learning environment

Did you know that listening to Mozart in the classroom has been shown to enhance a child's ability to learn effectively? Or that having water available to drink throughout lesson time has been shown to raise achievement? The unfathomable world of educational research! But there's a valuable lesson here if we're serious about helping the children in our churches to learn. The learning environment matters. Why have so many churches taken to removing pews and replacing them with chairs? Is it purely about the versatility that chairs provide in relation to pews, or is it also about the comfort of the congregation? Believe it or not, the building and the room you use to meet with your 8–10s can and will have a direct impact on how they learn.

Chapter Link

We've thought here about the kinds of resources that will enhance your learning environment. Look in Chapter Five for resources to support your planning and teaching of sessions.

Throughout the Bible, God has had little time for those who appear religious but are not concerned with the welfare of those around them. Look at:

- Isaiah 58:6,7
- Matthew 25:31–45
- James 1:27

What effect should our Christian faith have on the way we care for children, the way we treat leaders, the environment we work in and the procedures we adopt?

But there's nothing I can do...

Few churches have premises purpose-built for their work with children and young people – although if your church has the privilege of starting from scratch, or is in the midst of a building project, it's worth getting involved at the planning stage and staking your claim for facilities that at least take the needs of the children into account. However, most churches have at least got areas set aside for various children's and young people's groups to meet. So let's not simply sit back and dream about purpose-built premises, let's consider how to use the space you do have in a way that enhances the learning that takes place in your group.

You may think the area you have is far from ideal – but if it's what you've got then your commitment to making the best of it will speak volumes to your group. A few basics can make a world of difference. A key principle is to think about how you can make the environment suit the learning activities you want to offer the children, rather than letting your environment limit what you do. Obviously this isn't always possible but it's a positive and constructive approach!

Let's take a standard programme for an hour's teaching on a Sunday morning. Applying the principle of employing a range of teaching and learning styles to address the needs of your group, your programme might include a game, a discussion, a craft and some drama. Within such a programme space for a game and some drama needs to be combined with tables and chairs for the craft activity and a smaller, more intimate space for the discussion. A large room with clearly defined areas for each of these is of course the ideal – and rarely the reality! But there are solutions.

Who is going to help me?

Your group itself is an important resource here. Children are amazingly versatile and can become very adept at furniture moving! Show them how to transform a room prepared with chairs and tables into a space for a game or some drama and suddenly your far from ideal environment begins to look a little bit more manageable.

What else can I do?

Displaying children's work can be time-consuming if it's done properly, but there are three reasons why it's worth doing:

- It demonstrates that you value the work the children have done.
- It reinforces key teaching points.

And, particularly relevant here,

- It makes the learning environment look more attractive.

A fairly bleak and uninviting room can be personalised quite easily by free-standing or permanent notice boards with displays related to the teaching material being used. Keep displays up-to-date and relevant and the children will want to look at them, and will feel that the room they are in is personal to them, even if it has a multitude of other uses throughout the rest of the week.

Try, if you possibly can, to provide tables and chairs that are the right height for the children in your group. Educational suppliers are the best place to start, since they naturally provide custom-made furniture. And of course, such furniture will be more manageable for the children to move around in your versatile learning environment!

Beanbags are an enduring favourite and are ideal for providing the more intimate setting you might want to use for a discussion or prayer time. Involve the children in choosing them, or get them to choose some material and find some church members who can make them for the group.

The key really is simplicity. It's not so much about style and design as making sure that the children have the right furniture for the kinds of activities you plan into your programme. What you buy and how you arrange it in the room says a great deal about the kind of group you are.

Draw a plan of the room you work in with your group:

Now annotate your drawing – note the good and bad points of the learning environment. Think about:

- the arrangement of furniture.
- the suitability of furniture.
- storage of equipment.
- display space.
- any other factors.

Now write down two changes you could make to improve the learning environment – and put them into practice!

Chapter Eight – In a Perfect World…

The kingdom of heaven is like this…

When Jesus walked the earth, teaching people about following him, he told them many stories which began, 'The kingdom of heaven is like this…' Why? In today's 'business speak', we would say he wanted to share the vision. He wanted to enthuse his hearers, to excite them with glimpses of what life could be like. What makes his stories so exciting is that, although the characters and settings he uses are very ordinary and earthbound, we know that he is talking about a reality that we can share in. His stories are not pie in the sky, they are heaven on earth.

We believe that when we begin to feel a bit bogged down by the weight of things to do, meetings to arrange, volunteers to find, programmes to initiate and resources to make, it does our spirits good to tell stories, to dream dreams – because we know we have a God 'who is able to do immeasurably more than all we ask or imagine…' (Ephesians 3:20 NIV)!

So dream with us…

The children's work in the kingdom of heaven is like this…

Safe

The rooms used by all ages are appropriate to their needs. There is space to charge around and let off steam. There are comfortable seats, or maybe beanbags, which don't look too much like being at school. The activities are properly resourced, with pens that don't smell, glue which washes off clothing, balls which are soft, and hygienic conditions for preparing and eating food. There is a trained first-aider nearby, a mobile phone available to summon help and a fire drill which is practised regularly. The leaders are properly supported and held accountable, and there are well known procedures for following up any problems felt by children, leaders or parents. Children feel safe and secure because good behaviour is expected and rewarded, but those who are different are welcomed and supported too. This is a place where they can be real, vulnerable and honest without getting hurt.

Creative

The climate encourages all the children to have a go. They are tolerant of each other, and genuinely encouraging. They paint, dance, sing, make music, do drama and play games. Sometimes their efforts are private, just for themselves or to share with the group. Sometimes their work is offered as part of the whole church family's sacrifice of praise. Sometimes their creativity challenges the congregation, their spontaneity inspires them, and it is through them that we all see a glimpse of God.

Involved

The children know intuitively that others at church care for them. Whether they have come with their own family or not, they are used to others getting them a drink after the service, looking after them if they get hurt, asking how their exam went or complimenting them on a new haircut. They also expect that others will sometimes ask them to be quiet, or to sit down and listen, or that they will be asked to fetch a drink for someone else.

Practical

They can make a difference to where they live, and to people far away. They don't feel powerless and overlooked, because their suggestions for action are taken seriously. They might sponsor a child overseas and write to him regularly, run an 'alternative tuckshop' where all the sweets and chocolate are fair traded, form working parties to tackle community and environmental issues and be on the committee for the after school club.

Witnessing

The midweek club is the place to be locally. It is well known for the activities it offers, the trips that are run, the parties, tournaments and crafts. Parents are happy for their children to be there because it is properly staffed and they are kept well informed. Many of them are involved in transport or sharing their skills. It is attractive to unchurched children because it doesn't dodge the issues that concern them or give trite answers, but they know that the people they meet there have something appealing about the way they live, and they keep coming back to find out about it.

Spirit-filled

These young people are all going places with God. Some have only just put a foot on the path, others are experienced travellers, but there is an excitement about their worship and prayer that would be an eye-opener to many mature Christians. When they pray, they expect God to answer. They read the Bible because it tells them how to think and how to live. They sing because they can't help praising God, and they love to make up new songs, to dance and to make music for their Lord. They learn not just from what their leaders say, but from how they live, and their leaders have the humility to learn from them too.

Working with
8-10s

claire Saunders
& Hilary Porritt

For Andy: your unfailing optimism, love and encouragement kept me going! Thank you for everything.

For David: thank you for your love, your belief in me and your professional expertise and experience.

Acknowledgements

So many have helped us to write this book, through their prayers, words of encouragement and expertise. Thank you to all of you:

Kev Vaughan; Helen Franklin; Andy Richbell; Sharon Prior; Ruth Wills; Jilly Rowland; St John's Church, Boscombe, especially Rev Godfrey Taylor; the staff and children of Bethany Church of England Junior School, Epiphany Church of England Primary School and Stourfield Junior School; Tom, Emma and Sarah.

© Claire Saunders and Hilary Porritt 2004
First published 2004
ISBN 1 85999 661 2

Scripture Union, 207–209 Queensway, Bletchley, MK2 2EB, England.
Email: info@scriptureunion.org.uk
Website: www.scriptureunion.org.uk

Scripture Union Australia
Locked Bag 2, Central Coast Business Centre, NSW 2252
Website: www.su.org.au

Scripture Union USA
PO Box 987, Valley Forge, PA 19482
Website: www.scriptureunion.org

Scripture Union is an international Christian charity working with churches in more than 130 countries, providing resources to bring the good news about Jesus Christ to children, young people and families and to encourage them to develop spiritually through the Bible and prayer. As well as our network of volunteers, staff and associates who run holidays, church-based events and school Christian groups, we produce a wide range of publications and support those who use our resources through training programmes.

All rights reserved. The right-hand activity pages in this publication may be photocopied for use without reference to the current copyright legislation or any copyright licensing. This arrangement does not allow the printing of any of the other published material in permanent form. Nor does it allow the printing of words or illustrations for resale or for commercial use. Outside of this provision, no part of this publication may be reproduced, stored in a retrieval system, or transmitted, in any form or by any means, electronic, mechanical, photocopying, recording or otherwise, without the prior permission of Scripture Union.

The right of Claire Saunders and Hilary Porritt to be identified as authors of this work has been asserted by them in accordance with the Copyright, Designs and Patents Act 1988.

Unless otherwise stated, Bible quotations are taken from the Contemporary English Version ©American Bible Society 1991, 1992, 1995. Anglicisations ©British and Foreign Bible Society 1996. Published in the UK by HarperCollins Publishers and used with permission.

Material on pages 65, 67 and 69 taken from *Stop it or else!* by Kathryn Burgin, available from Scripture Union Field Ministries.

British Library Cataloguing-in-Publication Data.A catalogue record for this book is available from the British Library.

Printed and bound in Great Britain by Ebenezer Baylis and Sons Ltd.
Cover: Phil Grundy
Internal design and layout: 3T Creative
Illustrations: Ian West at Beehive Illustrations
Photographs: Silhouettes of kids in motion, Rubberball productions copyright © 2002